John the Baptist w.

John the Baptist
who became Jesus the Christ

Anne-Marie Wegh

MAGDALENA
PUBLISHERS

Table of contents

Introduction

My intention with everything I write is to arouse enthusiasm for a process of spiritual transformation that leads to a unification with God. An important question to me with the production of this book was: How will it affect the reader when I meddle with the Divine status of Jesus?

For Jews and "heathens" in the time of Jesus it was important to be able to see him as the Son of God. However, this same Divine status constitutes for many people nowadays a religious challenge. Someone who is born of a virgin and walks on water; few people can still accept that. And as Son of God, Jesus is far removed from the spiritual seeker. It is difficult to compare yourself to a perfect God-man. This is one of the reasons why his mother Mary is sometimes more popular among believers than Jesus: as woman of flesh and blood she is much closer to us.

With this book I want to bring Jesus back to human proportions, so that he can be for us what he wanted to be: an example of how we can actualize the Kingdom of God within ourselves.
After a process of self-emptying he realized a complete unification with God (John 10:30, John 17:21-22). In Biblical terms: he made of himself a temple for God to live in. He overcame the world (John 16:33) and became an anointed one, a Christ.

Jesus was human being who became so intimate with God that he called Him Father. That's something a modern spiritual seeker can relate to. That inspires imitation. And that is what Jesus wanted.

Jesus' deeds, his teachings, his death and resurrection, are unique in human history. That he began his life under a different name, takes nothing away from that.
I have written this book out of love and deep respect for the life story of the greatest human being ever.

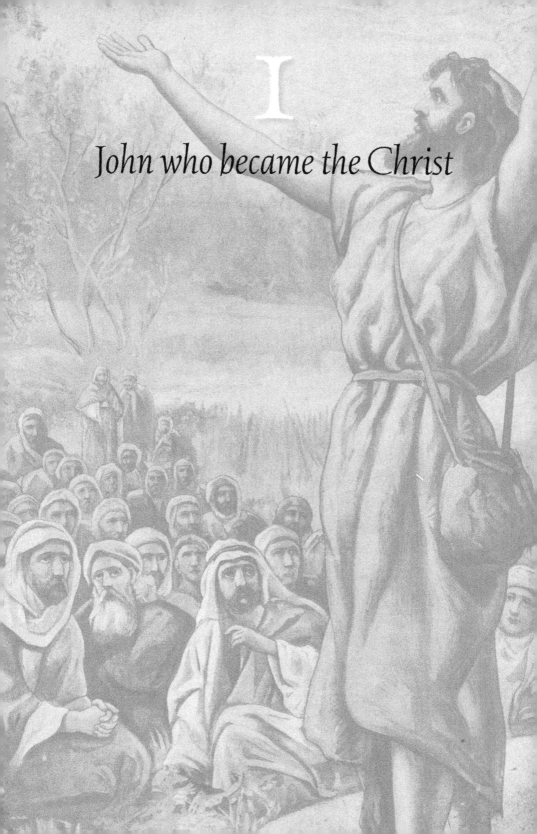

I

John who became the Christ

And the light shines in darkness; and the darkness comprehended it not.
There was a man sent from God, whose name was John.
The same came for a witness, to bear witness of the Light,
that all men through him might believe.

John 1:5-7 (KJV)

For two thousand years John the Baptist has been seen as the one who first predicted the coming of the Messiah and then recognized Jesus as "the Lamb of God" at his baptism in the Jordan River. Thus he is presented in the Bible, and with that John fulfilled the expectations of the Jews, who, based on the prophecies of Malachi, assumed that the long expected Messiah would be preceded by a great prophet.

John the Baptist, however, was not merely the herald of Jesus. He *was* Jesus. He became a *Christos*, an anointed one, after his process of God-realization, symbolized by the baptism in the Jordan. In this chapter I will show how this explosive supposition is covertly inserted in the gospel stories.

John the ascetic

In the gospels John the Baptist is described as an ascetic who lived in the wilderness and who wore clothing made of camel hair. He called upon people to repent and to be baptized by him. When Jesus wants to be baptized, John recognizes him as the Son of God:

> *The next day John saw Jesus coming toward him and said, "Look, the Lamb of God, who takes away the sin of the world!*
> *This is the one I meant when I said, 'A man who comes after me has surpassed me because he was before me.'*
> *I myself did not know him, but the reason I came baptizing with water was that he might be revealed to Israel."*
> *Then John gave this testimony: "I saw the Spirit come down from heaven as a dove and remain on him.*
> *And I myself did not know him, but the one who sent me to baptize with water told me, 'The man on whom you see the Spirit come down and remain is the one who will baptize with the Holy Spirit.'*
> *I have seen and I testify that this is the Son of God."*
> (John 1:29-34)

In reality Jesus and John were the same person. After a long process of purification, a unification with God occurs within John. He continues his life – at least in the gospels – by a new name: Jesus the Christ.

St. John the Baptist, by Bernardo Strozzi, 1620.
Accademia ligustica di Belle Arti, Genoa, Italy.

John has the *Ecce Agnus Dei-*banner in his hand and points at himself.

He has become the Messiah, for whom the Jews had anxiously waited all those many centuries. But this Savior was expected to fulfill a large number of prophecies from the Jewish Holy Scriptures. All evangelists, therefore, have permeated their stories with references to, and quotations from the Scriptures, to convince the reader that Jesus of Nazareth was the predicted Messiah.

John the Baptist did not satisfy these prophecies. Moreover, as Jesus himself attests in all four of the gospels, a prophet is never honored in his own hometown:
Jesus said to them, "A prophet is not without honor except in his own town,

among his relatives and in his own home." He could not do any miracles there, except lay his hands on a few sick people and heal them. He was amazed at their lack of faith.
(Mark 6:4-6, also see Matt. 13:57, Luke 4:24 and John 4:44)

Jesus could not perform any miracles where people already knew him. It's difficult for people to acknowledge someone with whom they grew up as prophet, let alone as Messiah. Even his brothers, who traveled with him, doubted him:

Jesus' brothers said to him, "Leave Galilee and go to Judea, so that your disciples there may see the works you do.
No one who wants to become a public figure acts in secret. Since you are doing these things, show yourself to the world."
For even his own brothers did not believe in him.
(John 7:3-5)

That's remarkable. According to the gospels, his coming as Messiah had been announced by an angel prior to his birth to both his father and his mother. He was also supernaturally conceived. At the age of twelve he caused quite a stir in the temple of Jerusalem with his wisdom (Luke 2:41-52). His brothers, however, don't believe in him?

This reaction of the environment and the family of Jesus fits a man who did not begin his life as Son of God, but as an ordinary human being, like us. Like John the Baptist.

Before we will have a look at how the various evangelists handled the John-is-Jesus-secret, first a brief elucidation of the illustrations in this chapter.

In works of art
Through the ages there has been a small group of free spirits, artists and mystics who guarded the secret that John the Baptist was Jesus. I have identified a large number of paintings from the 15th century and later, with pointers to John and Jesus being the same person. A number of works of art are shown

Madonna with Child, a Bishop and John The Baptist, by Antonio da Firenze, 15th century.
Hermitage museum, St. Petersburg.

John holds the *Ecce Agnus Dei-*banner in his hand and points not to Jesus but to himself.
Mary and her child look at John.

14

in this chapter, and an additional selection appears in the appendix. There are, however, many more.

The pointers are usually subtle. The church was an important employer to many artists, and they could not afford to openly question established dogma. John and Jesus the same person ... that would have been intolerable! The large amount of paintings with a John-is-Jesus code, and the variations with which the theme is tackled, gives the impression of a certain delight on the part of the artists with exploring the forbidden subject.

The John-is-Jesus-code

Traditionally, John is depicted as an ascetic with a robe of camel hair, pointing with his finger to Jesus. Often he carries a banner with the words *Ecce Agnus Dei*, which means "See the Lamb of God"; the words which John uttered when Jesus approached him to be baptized by him (John 1:29).

The artists who incorporated the John-is-Jesus-message in their paintings made use of devices and alterations to traditional iconography that include:

-   John and Jesus look nearly identical (pages 18, 156, 159, 162, 163, 166, 168, 174, 176, 183, 190).
-   John carries the *Ecce Agnus Dei*-banner ("See the Lamb of God") but points to himself instead of to Jesus, as if to say: *I* am the Lamb of God (pages 12, 14, 167, 169, 179, 180).
-   John carries a wooden cross with the *Ecce Agnus Dei*-banner missing, which connects him to the crucifixion (pages 18, 154, 157, 163, 164, 165, 166, 170, 171, 173, 182, 183, 184, 185, 187, 188, 189, 191, 193, 194, 195).
-   Jesus points to John instead of the other way around, or they point at each other (pages 18, 156, 159, 171).
-   John, Jesus and/or one of the others on the painting display with their hands **the 2=1-code:** someone on the painting raises two fingers and (someone else) one finger. In other words: the two persons are in reality one (pages 16, 24, 153, 155, 162, 164, 198, and the cover of this book).
-   The others on the painting look at John instead of (the infant) Jesus. Anachronism is customary in paintings of this era: for example, John is depicted as a grown man and Jesus as child (pages 26, 184).

15

A pieta composition with various saints, by Andrea Lilli, first half of the 17th century. Private collection, Bagnacavallo, Italy.

John points with one finger to Jesus and with two fingers to himself (the 2=1-code).

- John is displayed in a fashion that gives him the appearance of Jesus (pages 32, 154, 191, 193).
- The dove of the Holy Spirit hovers over John instead of Jesus at the baptism, or is positioned between them (pages 173, 174, 175, 177, 178, 198).

The gospel of Luke

The evangelist Luke gives us the most details of the life of John. Because of this gospel John is generally seen as the cousin of Jesus, but this is not confirmed by the other three evangelists. Luke opens his gospel with the annunciation of the birth of John by the angel Gabriel to the priest Zechariah. When we look at chapter 1 with the right kind of eyes, the message of Gabriel about John could easily be construed to be about his future life as Jesus the Christ:

> But the angel said to him: "Do not be afraid, Zechariah; your prayer has been heard. Your wife Elizabeth will bear you a son, and you are to call him John. He will be a joy and delight to you, and many will rejoice because of his birth, for he will be great in the sight of the Lord. He is never to take wine or other fermented drink, and he will be filled with the Holy Spirit even before he is born.
> He will bring back many of the people of Israel to the Lord their God.
> And he will go on before the Lord, in the spirit and power of Elijah, to turn the hearts of the parents to their children and the disobedient to the wisdom of the righteous—to make ready a people prepared for the Lord."
> (Luke 1:13-17)

The pregnancy of Elizabeth is special because she is advanced in years and appears to have been infertile thus far (Luke 1:7). With that Luke places John on the list of other remarkable pregnancies in the Old Testament and makes his birth even more special. Patriarch Abraham and his wife Sarah were advanced in years when they were given a son: Isaac. Isaac's wife Rebekah appeared to be initially barren but then, upon God's intervention, had two sons Jacob and Esau.

Then there are Rachel and the wife of Manoah who had sons only after a long period of infertility. Hence all these births demonstrated the favor and

17

Madonna of Casalmaggiore (copy), by Antonio Allegri, also known as Correggio, ca 1522.
Städelsches Kunstinstitut Und Städtische Galerie, Frankfurt.

Jesus and John look the same and point to each other. Mary looks at John.
John holds a wooden cross without a banner.

grace of God, which in turn fell upon the whole of Israel. Luke deliberately places John in this honored gallery of great names. Additionally he submits impressive genealogical information:

> In the time of Herod king of Judea there was a priest named Zechariah, who belonged to the priestly division of Abijah; his wife Elizabeth was also a descendant of Aaron.
> Both of them were righteous in the sight of God, observing all the Lord's commands and decrees blamelessly.
> (Luke 1:5-6)

Someone's descent was to the Jews in that time very important. The family lineage of both Zechariah and Elizabeth traces back to the very first high priest Aaron, the brother of Moses. An enviable business card!

Zechariah, Elizabeth and the birth of John are not mentioned by the other evangelists. With them John enters the stage at the baptism of Jesus. Luke, however, spends almost as many words on the birth and early years of John as on those of Jesus. The entire first chapter of Luke is in fact about John. The evangelist knows that John doesn't have the paperwork to be accepted as the Messiah, but he wants the truth to be found in his gospel, hidden behind a veil.

After the annunciation of the birth of John by Gabriel, Luke proceeds with the annunciation of the birth of Jesus to Mary by the same angel. The hidden meaning of this second birth is that it will come about *in* John: the birth of the Christ-child in his soul.

Pregnant by the Holy Spirit
Mary plays a varying symbolic role in the gospel stories; she represents the inner feminine on different levels. In the annunciation of the birth of Jesus she represents the soul (which has been regarded as feminine since antiquity).

The conception of the Christ-child will take place through the "overshadowing" of the Holy Spirit, says verse 35. Said otherwise: the Divine birth

Annunciation of the birth of Jesus

26 In the sixth month of Elizabeth's pregnancy, God sent the angel Gabriel to Nazareth, a town in Galilee,

27 to a virgin pledged to be married to a man named Joseph, a descendant of David. The virgin's name was Mary.

28 The angel went to her and said, "Greetings, you who are highly favored! The Lord is with you."

29 Mary was greatly troubled at his words and wondered what kind of greeting this might be.

30 But the angel said to her, "Do not be afraid, Mary; you have found favor with God.

31 You will conceive and give birth to a son, and you are to call him Jesus.

32 He will be great and will be called the Son of the Most High. The Lord God will give him the throne of his father David,

33 and he will reign over Jacob's descendants forever; his kingdom will never end."

34 "How will this be," Mary asked the angel, "since I am a virgin?"

35 The angel answered, "The Holy Spirit will come on you, and the power of the Most High will overshadow you. So the holy one to be born will be called the Son of God.

36 Even Elizabeth your relative is going to have a child in her old age, and she who was said to be unable to conceive is in her sixth month.

37 For no word from God will ever fail."

38 "I am the Lord's servant," Mary answered. "May your word to me be fulfilled." Then the angel left her.

(Luke 1:26-38)

in the soul (Mary) will be possible because the Holy Spirit will perform the necessary purifications. In the average spiritual aspirant this takes years rather than months. During this period one is "pregnant" by the Holy Spirit.

Mary will be pregnant and bear a son without having intercourse with a man (verse 34). This virgin birth – for twenty centuries a topic of heated debate – confirms that this is not about a physical but a spiritual birth.

Zechariah's song

In his first chapter, Luke has both Mary and Zechariah dedicate a long prayer of thanksgiving to God (see next page). During her visit to her cousin Elizabeth, Mary exclaims her famous song, which fittingly became known as "Mary's song"; an all time favorite with choirs and church goers.

Somewhat less familiar is Zechariah's song, which in length and poetic beauty is certainly not inferior to Maria's song. When we place the two texts next to each other, we notice that Zechariah explicitly mentions his child that will be born, but Mary makes no mention of a child. She speaks only about herself and the mercy she encountered!

Maria confirms the reason of this in her opening sentence: *My soul glorifies the Lord* ... Mary symbolizes the soul of a person in which God is born. In this case it's the soul of John but the gospels are written in such a way that the stories apply to every seeker of God. It will also be the song of praise of our soul when it is unified with God. A mystical marriage out of which the Divine child, the Christ-child, is born. A birth that can only transpire in a humble heart (verse 48). A heart like John's.

The trailblazer

A remarkable element of Zechariah's song is his statement that with the birth of his son God's promise to the patriarch Abraham is fulfilled (verse 73). Now finally the Messiah will come, who will liberate Israel from the (inner) enemy (verse 71) and who will lead the Jews onto an era of (inner) peace (verse 79).

People commonly assume that Zechariah refers to Jesus and that John will be his "trailblazer" or herald, but that is not what the text says. Verse 76 says

21

Mary's Song

46 And Mary said: "My soul glorifies the Lord

47 and my spirit rejoices in God my Savior,

48 for he has been mindful of the humble state of his servant. From now on all generations will call me blessed,

49 for the Mighty One has done great things for me – holy is his name.

50 His mercy extends to those who fear him, from generation to generation.

51 He has performed mighty deeds with his arm; he has scattered those who are proud in their inmost thoughts.

52 He has brought down rulers from their thrones but has lifted up the humble.

53 He has filled the hungry with good things but has sent the rich away empty.

54 He has helped his servant Israel, remembering to be merciful

55 to Abraham and his descendants forever, just as he promised our ancestors."

(Luke 1:46-55)

Zechariah's Song

67 His father Zechariah was filled with the Holy Spirit and prophesied:

68 "Praise be to the Lord, the God of Israel, because he has come to his people and redeemed them.

69 He has raised up a horn of salvation for us in the house of his servant David

70 (as he said through his holy prophets of long ago),

71 salvation from our enemies and from the hand of all who hate us—

72 to show mercy to our ancestors and to remember his holy covenant,

73 the oath he swore to our father Abraham:

74 to rescue us from the hand of our enemies, and to enable us to serve him without fear

75 in holiness and righteousness before him all our days.

76 And you, my child, will be called a prophet of the Most High; for you will go on before the Lord to prepare the way for him,

77 to give his people the knowledge of salvation through the forgiveness of their sins,

78 because of the tender mercy of our God, by which the rising sun will come to us from heaven

79 to shine on those living in darkness and in the shadow of death, to guide our feet into the path of peace."

(Luke 1:67-79)

that John will prepare the way for the Most High. Through inner purification and the denouncing of his ego, John will pave the road for God himself.

Below we will see that also the other evangelists have made use of the image of John as the trailblazer of God, which can be explained in two different ways.

All authors hint in their texts that we must interpret this task of John as an internal, spiritual process; a path he himself walked and which he wanted to show us. *To shine on those living in darkness and in the shadow of death* (verse 79), is about shining on people whose consciousness is unenlightened; all who are dead in the spiritual sense.

After Zechariah's song, Luke concludes with words about John, which again can be explained in two ways:

> *And the child grew and became strong in spirit; and he lived in the wilderness until he appeared publicly to Israel.*
> (Luke 1:80)

This can be read as: John lived in the wilderness until he went to work as baptist and converter. But this can also be read as: John lived in the wilderness until he – after his spiritual transformation – appeared to the people of Israel as Jesus the Christ.

The description "he appeared publicly to Israel" matches in my view better someone who comes out of nowhere and goes public as the Messiah, than someone who starts to baptize people in the Jordan. And when we have a look at the deeper meaning of a stay in *the wilderness*, the second interpretation becomes even more likely.

The wilderness
It's not very probable that we should take this literal: a child that grows up by himself in the wilderness, or desert, which is also one of the translations of the Greek word *érèmos*. *Érèmos* literally means abandonment. It may refer to a place, but also to a person. For instance an abandoned wife

John the Baptist, by Leonardo da Vinci, 1513-1516.
The Louvre Museum, Paris.

John point to himself with two fingers of his left hand (the 2=1-code).

or abandoned animals: a herd of sheep without a shepherd. When the word *érèmos* is used in the Bible, the author usually wants to say something about someone's inner world: like a desert. An arid, dry place where the heavens remain closed. A wilderness; a place where wild animals live and the laws are those of the jungle.

With a childhood in the wilderness, Luke wants to tell us that John spent the first segment of his life severed from God, just like all other people.

All four evangelists write that John, once an adult, also *preached* in the wilderness (Mark 1:3-4, Matt. 3:1-3, Luke 3:4 and John 1:23). Whoever senses a call to convert others isn't going to do that in a wilderness, you would think, but in places where lots of people are. Again a hint that we may regard *érèmos* figuratively. After he himself had found God, John addressed everybody who was severed from Him, everybody who was living in spiritual isolation.

The gospels write about John: "a voice calling in the wilderness," after the words of the prophet Isaiah:

> ³ A voice of one calling:
> "In the wilderness prepare
> the way for the Lord;
> make straight in the desert
> a highway for our God.
> ⁴ Every valley shall be raised up,
> every mountain and hill made low;
> the rough ground shall become level,
> the rugged places a plain.
> ⁵ And the glory of the Lord will be revealed,
> and all people will see it together.
> For the mouth of the Lord has spoken."
> (Isaiah 40:3-5)

Madonna del Ceppo, by Filippo Lippi, 1453.
Palazzo Pretorio Museum, Prato, Italië.

The characters left on the painting all look in adoration at John, instead of the infant Jesus.
John shows the *Ecce Agnus Dei*-banner without pointing toward Jesus.

You can understand these words in two ways. The traditional interpretation is that John calls to repentance, with the coming of Jesus in mind.

You can also read it as a call for inner purification, for clearing out everything that stands between God and man, for the leveling of everything that makes the path to His Kingdom rough and impassable. So that in us: *the glory of the Lord will be revealed* (verse 5). A call to, just like John, prepare the way for the birth of the Divine child in our soul.

The baptism in the Jordan

Apart from a visit to the temple of Jerusalem when Jesus was twelve years old and during which he greatly impressed the adults who were present there (an event which only Luke reports; 2:41-52), the gospels are silent about the childhood of Jesus. His public life begins with the baptism in the Jordan.

When we review what the four evangelists wrote about this crucial moment, something remarkable jumps out. The gospel of Luke only reports that Jesus was baptized but not by whom. And in the other three gospels – Matthew, Mark and John – John the Baptist never mentions the name Jesus, but speaks of "He who comes after me."

This vague description must leave room for the true meaning of baptism: the inner transformation of John himself. The ego of John will make way for God (*He who comes after me*), after which he will continue his life in the Bible as Jesus the Christ.

> *I baptize you with water for repentance. But after me comes one who is more powerful than I, whose sandals I am not worthy to carry. He will baptize you with the Holy Spirit and fire.*
> (Matt. 3:11)

The birth of Jesus

But what about the stories of the nativity of Jesus in the gospels of Matthew and Luke? With the manger and the shepherds and the Magi from the east? The birth of the Christ-child that we commemorate every Christmas in word and image?

The two stories of Jesus' birth should not be read as a historic report, but as a metaphor for the birth of the Divine in every human person. That's why the story of Luke differs in almost every detail with that of Matthew[1].

The Christmas story transpires within anyone who chooses the path to God and perseveres to the end. It is the journey which Mary and Joseph make to Bethlehem: "the place from whence they came" (read: God). It is also the journey which the Magi from the east undertake, in order to regard the Christ-child with their own eyes. The gifts they bear correspond to the spiritual gifts which we receive when the Divine is born within us.

John the Baptist captured

In all three of the synoptic gospels – Matthew, Mark and Luke – the ministry of Jesus commences when John exits the stage upon his capture by King Herod:

> When Jesus heard that John had been put in prison, he withdrew to Galilee. **From that time on** Jesus began to preach, "Repent, for the kingdom of heaven has come near."
> (Matt. 4:12 and 17; also see Mark 1:14-15 and Luke 3:19-21)

Matthew tells us covertly that Jesus is the born-again John, by having them say the same words. The first public words of Jesus are: *Repent, for the kingdom of heaven has come near* (Matt. 4:17). John says the same in verse 3:2. And both call the hypocritical Pharisees "brood of vipers!" John in verse 3:7 and Jesus in verses 12:34 and 23:33.

An interesting and much revealing passage is the moment in which Jesus asks his disciples who the people think he is:

> When Jesus came to the region of Caesarea Philippi, he asked his disciples, "Who do people say the Son of Man is?"
> They replied, "Some say **John the Baptist**; others say Elijah; and still others, Jeremiah or one of the prophets."
> "But what about you?" he asked. "Who do you say I am?"

Simon Peter answered, "You are the Messiah, the Son of the living God."
Jesus replied, "Blessed are you, Simon son of Jonah, for this was not revealed to
you by flesh and blood, but by my Father in heaven.
(Matt. 16:13-17)

Matthew states in no uncertain terms that there were people in those days
who thought that Jesus was John the Baptist. Elijah and Jeremiah are prophets from the Old Testament, and it is plausible that people saw Jesus as
reincarnation of one of them. But why would people say he was John the
Baptist? In the gospels they are portrayed as two entirely different men, with
a wholly individual conversion method. The simple answer is: because he
indeed was John the Baptist!

The gospel of John

In the gospel of John (which was of course not named after John the Baptist but after the apostle John), the evangelist sets a slightly different course
with regard to the John-Jesus question. He opens his gospel with John the
Baptist, who came to testify of the light (see next page). The traditional
interpretation of this dictates that the Baptist merely identified Jesus as the
Son of God. But the opening words may also be read differently, that John
came to testify of the light of God that lived within him.

What strikes is that John is mentioned twice in the impressive and much
quoted first eighteen verses, and Jesus only once. Intuitively this doesn't
appear to match the importance of these individuals in the story.

After the poetic opening, Jewish priests and Levites show up right away in
verse 1:20 to ask John the burning question that is central in this book:

"...Who art thou?"
And he confessed, and denied not; but confessed, "I am not the Christ."
(John 1:19-20, KJV)

The formulation of his answer is remarkable: a confirmation directly followed by a negation. Biblical exegetes view this as a literary style: an em-

The Gospel according to John

1 In the beginning was the Word, and the Word was with God, and the Word was God.

2 He was with God in the beginning.

3 Through him all things were made; without him nothing was made that has been made.

4 In him was life, and that life was the light of all mankind.

5 The light shines in the darkness, and the darkness has not overcome it.

6 There was a man sent from God whose name was John.

7 He came as a witness to testify concerning that light, so that through him all might believe.

8 He himself was not the light; he came only as a witness to the light.

9 The true light that gives light to everyone was coming into the world.

10 He was in the world, and though the world was made through him, the world did not recognize him.

11 He came to that which was his own, but his own did not receive him.

12 Yet to all who did receive him, to those who believed in his name, he gave the right to become children of God—

13 children born not of natural descent, nor of human decision or a husband's will, but born of God.

14 The Word became flesh and made his dwelling among us. We have seen his glory, the glory of the one and only Son, who came from the Father, full of grace and truth.

15 (John testified concerning him. He cried out, saying, "This is the one I spoke about when I said, 'He who comes after me has surpassed me because he was before me.'")

16 Out of his fullness we have all received grace in place of grace already given.

17 For the law was given through Moses; grace and truth came through Jesus Christ.

18 No one has ever seen God, but the one and only Son, who is himself God and is in closest relationship with the Father, has made him known.

(John 1:1-18)

phatic denial. I think, however, that it is a method of the author to inform us covertly that John was indeed the Christ!

In addition, this evangelist places John twice "*on the other side of the Jordan*". "The other side" is a classic metaphor for transformation.

> *This all happened at Bethany on the other side of the Jordan, where John was baptizing.*
> (John 1:28)

> *They came to John and said to him, "Rabbi, that man who was with you on the other side of the Jordan – the one you testified about – look, he is baptizing, and everyone is going to him."*
> (John 3:26)

Interestingly, some versions of this Gospel give in verse 1:28 Bethabara as the place where John baptized, instead of Bethany. Beth-abara means *place of crossing*.

Jesus the Baptist

In the New Testament, Jesus is called the Nazorene (Greek: *Nazōraios*). Exegetes don't generally agree on how this epithet should be translated. The Bible translates it as Jesus of Nazareth, or as Jesus the Nazarene, but a town called Nazareth did not exist at that time. In this mysterious word *Nazōraios* is hidden the secret of John who became Jesus.

Etymology
The Greek word *Nazōraios* probably stems from the Hebrew *nazar*, and might as such be translated as "someone who consecrates." Consecration can take place through baptism.

Someone who baptizes could be called a *Nazōraios*. With this appears a possible translation of *Iēsous ho Nazōraios* as: Jesus the Baptist!

The successor of John the Baptist is Jesus the Baptist, and this born-again human being no longer baptizes with water but with the Holy Spirit:

The Sermon of St. John the Baptist, by Bernardo Strozzi, ca 1644.
Kunsthistorisches Museum, Vienna.

John looks like Jesus. He loosely holds on to the *Ecce Agnus Dei* banner, without pointing at anyone. One of the audience motions with one hand toward John and with the other upward, as if he means to say, "This is the Lamb of God."

32

And this was his message: "After me comes the one more powerful than I, the straps of whose sandals I am not worthy to stoop down and untie.
I baptize you with water, but he will baptize you with the Holy Spirit."
(Mark 1:7-8)

Nazareth a fictional town?
Nazareth is probably a fictional town, made up to mask Jesus' moniker the Nazorene, to prevent that a connection would be made with John the Baptist. No other source contemporary with the New Testament makes mention of a village with the name Nazareth. Neither the Old Testament, nor the epistles of the apostles mention Nazareth. Only the gospels speak of Nazareth as the home town of Jesus. In the gospel of Matthew we read about Joseph, the father of Jesus:

and he went and lived in a town called Nazareth. So was fulfilled what was said through the prophets, that he would be called a Nazarene.
(Matt. 2:23)

However, nowhere in the Old Testament is stated that the Messiah would be called a Nazarene. Moreover, the Greek source text of above quote says that he would be called a Nazorene (*Nazōraíos*).

In order to covertly confirm to us that Jesus the Nazorene refers to John the Baptist, Matthew proceeds right after verse 2:23 with the introduction of John the Baptist:

In those days John the Baptist came, preaching in the wilderness of Judea and saying, "Repent, for the kingdom of heaven has come near."
(Matt. 3:1-2)

Greek versus Hebrew
Because the name of John the Baptist is written in the gospels in Greek – Iōannēs ho Baptistēs – and not in Hebrew, no one, as far as I am aware, has noticed that both Jesus and John are referred to as "the Baptist."

The evangelists have concealed this even further through the fictional hometown Nazareth, because of which the nickname Jesus the Nazorene became interpreted as referring to the city in which he grew up.

In the next chapter we will learn more about the nature of the spiritual process that transformed John the Baptist to the God-realized man Jesus.

2

The Bible, a guide to spiritual awakening

For we are the temple of the living God. As God has said:
"I will live with them and walk among them,
and I will be their God, and they will be my people."

2 Corinthians 6:16

The Bible can be regarded in several distinct ways. Many readers prefer to take the stories of the Bible literal and aim to live their lives according to the example of Jesus and the instructions he left us. Others see the Bible as a wholly human product and study it scientifically and anthropologically, or admire it as the great depository of narrative archetypes that still carries artistic expressions today. Many, however, have abandoned the Bible and seek solace in Far Eastern traditions.

I want to show you an additional and exiting way to look at the Bible. We will have a close look at the stories of the Old and New Testament, and discover amazing parallels between the stories of the Bible and the principles of Hinduism. We will see a universal and guiding message emerge; hidden in gruesome stories about war, slavery and animal sacrifice, we will find a roadmap to self-actualization and spiritual awakening.

The deeper layers of the Bible rise to the surface when we review the figurative and symbolic qualities of the Biblical stories. They teach us how we can realize the Kingdom of God. Not after death, somewhere in another dimension, but here and now on earth, within ourselves; how we can make of ourselves a temple for God to live in.

Who was Jesus?
The central inquiry of this book is: who was Jesus? In order to understand what the gospels say about him, not only some knowledge of symbolism is required but also of the basic principles of kundalini-awakening. Many of the Bible stories center on a process of spiritual rebirth, in which a mysterious source of energy in our pelvis plays the main role[2]. This energy source of Divine origin is called *kundalini-shakti* in eastern traditions. The New Testament calls it the Holy Spirit.

Jesus himself experienced a kundalini-awakening and wanted to teach us how we too may become worthy of this Divine initiation.

In this chapter we will first review the basic principles of the kundalini-process. After this we will unravel the symbolism of a particular story from the Old Testament and one from the New Testament, and finish with a review

Kundalini-awakening: the seven chakras and the three nadis.

of several examples of kundalini-symbolism in the stories relating to Jesus and John the Baptist.

Chakras, nadis and amrita

In the pelvis of every human being, at the level of the sacrum, slumbers an energetic power source of which in spiritual traditions the knowledge was shared only with a select group of initiated. One of the universal metaphors of this transcendental energy source is the serpent. The Sanskrit word *kundalini* means "coiled," which refers to the fact that with most people this "serpent" remains coiled up asleep (i.e. not active).

The image of the serpent, with its ability to renew itself by shedding its skin, represents the transforming aspect of the kundalini. Once active, the kundalini initiates a process of purification and healing, which results in a state of detachment, great inner peace, silence, and joy. This healing and self-emptying is a required condition for the next step in the process: the unification with God.

The kundalini can become active through deliberate spiritual exercise (meditation and prayer and such) but can also awaken spontaneously. Special exercises aren't really necessary and direct stimulation is not recommended. The kundalini becomes active when the spiritual aspirant is ready; when there is a genuine interest in growing toward God, a willingness to renounce the personal self, and when some level of purity has already been achieved at the level of the body, thought and action.

Inner equilibrium

The keyword concerning kundalini-awakening is *equilibrium*. At the left and right of our spinal column are located two important energy channels, which the yoga tradition calls *ida-* and *pingala-nadi*. These energy channels constitute the energetic blueprint of the duality in a human being. They represent the opposites, comparable to yin and yang of Taoism.

Where the *ida-nadi* represents the feminine, dark, cold, passivity and feeling, the *pingala-nadi* represents the masculine, light, warmth, activity and reason. The genders of these energy channels express archetypal opposites and have nothing to do with the gender of the individual. Every human being has an *ida-* and *pingala-nadi* and thus a masculine and a feminine side. The mission of the spiritual aspirant is to bring these energy channels into equilibrium. Then – and if God wills – the kundalini will awaken and rise from the pelvis through the *sushumna-nadi*, the energy channel which runs through the spinal column.

A physical symbol which appears frequently in the Bible is the scepter, rod or staff, which possesses magic or miraculous powers. This physical attribute, often in the possession of a Biblical hero, refers to the spinal column through which kundalini-energy freely flows. The prophet Moses, for instance, had such a staff, and with it he was able to perform miracles. He was able to transform it into a serpent (Ex 4:3). When he raised it, the Red Sea parted (Ex 14:21), and when he hit a rock with it, water poured forth (Ex 17:6)[3].

Trees and shrubs
Another much used metaphor of awakened kundalini-energy in the spinal column is a tree or shrub. The book of Genesis tells of the Garden of Eden with at its center the Tree of Life whose fruits give eternal life. In the New Testament we read in the parables of Jesus of trees that bear fruit, or that should if they don't. Even the very Kingdom of God, Jesus said, is like a mustard seed that grows into a large tree (Matt 13:31-32).

In kundalini symbolism the fig tree occupies a special place among the trees, not only in the Bible but also in Buddhism, Hinduism and ancient Egypt. In the gospel of Luke (19:1-6), Zacchaeus, whose name means "pure", climbs up a fig tree to see Jesus (i.e. God). At the end of this chapter we will discuss a striking example of a 19th century biblical painting in which kundalini symbolism is connected to the fig tree.

A purifying fire
Between the pelvis and the crown of one's head, along the spinal column, seven important energy centers are located, which in eastern traditions are called *chakras* (literally: wheels). On its way to the highest chakra – the

crown chakra – the transcendental fire of the kundalini purifies the six other chakras. On a psychological level, the ego is cleared of all its traumas, un-resolved emotions and unnecessary ballast, accumulated since childhood.

Although some traditions promote the death of the ego in order to achieve the Divine, it's better to speak of the pursuit of *transparency* of the ego. A personal "self" is purified to such a degree that it allows the Divine light to pass unhindered, like a clean window.

The sacred marriage

When the kundalini arrives at the sixth chakra, the *ida-* and *pingala-na-di* merge. On the forehead of the spiritual aspirant the so-called "third eye" opens. This merger between the masculine and feminine energies also leads to the opening of the crown chakra, and the unification of man and his Creator takes place. This is referred to as the "sacred marriage." Following this internal marriage, the Divine child – the Christ child – is born in our soul.

Also at the psychological level a transformation takes place: the ego is defi-nitely renounced; the old man "dies." The purified, new man experiences an expanded consciousness and subsequently a living connection with God. In Christian terms this is called being born again.

Amrita

This process also has an important *physical* component. Our human brain contains regions called the epiphysis (or pineal gland), the hypophysis and the hypothalamus whose job it is to excrete hormones and endogenous opi-ates. When the kundalini arrives at the crown chakra, these areas of the brain are stimulated into producing chemicals that contribute both to the experience of God and an overall vitalization of the body. Eastern traditions call these excreted substances *amrita*, which means "immortality". The Bible speaks of an "anointing" by the Holy Spirit.

Jesus the Christ

The deeper meaning of ancient anointing rituals is the transformation of brain fluids into *amrita*. The pouring of oil on the heads of kings and priests

Saul is anointed king

symbolizes the internal, spiritual process by which a person becomes an anointed one. This ritual is a remnant from the time that kings, priests, and prophets were assumed to be connected to the Divine.

The word *Messiah* stems from the Hebrew *Mashiah* and means "Anointed [one]"; someone who underwent an anointing ritual. The Greek word for this is *Christos*. This title is of course most obviously connected to Jesus the Christ of Nazareth but certainly not limited to him. In fact, every human has the ability to share in the anointing (1 John 2:27), that means to become a Messiah, an Anointed one, a Christ!

Our lower and higher nature

Humans have basically two natures: an animal nature that connects us to our biological origin, and a Divine nature that connect us to our potential destiny. Our actions are partly directed by our animal instincts (our lower nature), and partly by the longing for Divine union, which is the birthright of all humans (2 Peter 1:4).

This duality yields a continuous internal tension, whether we realize this or not. The impulses of our animal instincts, which are rooted in our body (2 Peter 2:12), are often posed perpendicular to the desires of our soul, which is connected to the Divine (Psalm 42).

Animals are capable of immense cruelty. Weaker individuals are cast out, rivals wounded, imperfect offspring killed. But their behavior is instinctual and serves to preserve the species. It is not the result of a freedom of choice. Humans on the other hand have the additional ability to discern between good and evil and to empathize with others.

This may tempt us to see ourselves as far above the primitive animal realm, but much of our behavior can be clearly derived from our animal heritage. Arbitrarily open up a magazine and you'll see that mankind is predominantly occupied with appearance (reminiscent of the flaunting and grooming of animals), sex and food. Watch sports games and you'll see sublimated battles for territory and rivalry. Also qualities such

Adam and Eve are clothed in animal skins and driven out of the Garden of Eden

as greed, aggression, jealousy and egoism are bestial tendencies. And let's not forget our herd mentality. Whoever isn't guilty of that may cast the first stone!

And through the chaos of our bestial tendencies, the gentle voice of our higher nature, seated in our hearts, calls us to compassion, servitude, justice and sharing with others.

When Adam and Eve were forced to leave Paradise, God clothed them in animal skins (Gen 3:21). This symbolizes what happens when we incarnate on earth. Man loses contact with his higher nature (Paradise, God) and receives in return a body with animal instincts. Virtually all Biblical stories about wars, tyrannical kings, cruel invaders and dashing heroes are descriptions of the universal battle within every human being: the clash between the hypnotic forces of his lower, animal nature, and the call of his higher, Divine nature.

The spiritual mission that every person is charged with is to conquer the bestial in order to realize the Divine potential. The key word here is "conquer". Our mission is not to suppress or deny – a seductive pitfall on our path – but to master. These very primal forces – though purified and sublimated – can help us to accomplish the higher, and the kundalini is a God-given instrument to achieve this.

We don't need to go this tough and long road alone; we do this together with our Creator. The kundalini is a holy fire that consumes everything that stands between us and the Divine.

Jesus and the Samaritan woman at the well

In the gospel of John we find the intriguing story of the encounter which Jesus had with a Samaritan woman at a well. Virtually all aspects of the kundalini process that we discuss in this chapter are incorporated into this story. It's an apt example to scrutinize, also because it features a character from the Old Testament.

Jesus Talks With a Samaritan Woman

1 Now Jesus learned that the Pharisees had heard that he was gaining and baptizing more disciples than John—

2 although in fact it was not Jesus who baptized, but his disciples.

3 So he left Judea and went back once more to Galilee.

4 Now he had to go through Samaria.

5 So he came to a town in Samaria called Sychar, near the plot of ground Jacob had given to his son Joseph.

6 Jacob's well was there, and Jesus, tired as he was from the journey, sat down by the well. It was about noon.

7 When a Samaritan woman came to draw water, Jesus said to her, "Will you give me a drink?"

8 (His disciples had gone into the town to buy food.)

9 The Samaritan woman said to him, "You are a Jew and I am a Samaritan woman. How can you ask me for a drink?" (For Jews do not associate with Samaritans.)

10 Jesus answered her, "If you knew the gift of God and who it is that asks you for a drink, you would have asked him and he would have given you living water."

11 "Sir," the woman said, "you have nothing to draw with and the well is deep. Where can you get this living water?

12 Are you greater than our father Jacob, who gave us the well and drank from it himself, as did also his sons and his livestock?"

13 Jesus answered, "Everyone who drinks this water will be thirsty again,

14 but whoever drinks the water I give them will never thirst. Indeed, the water I give them will become in them a spring of water welling up to eternal life."

15 The woman said to him, "Sir, give me this water so that I won't get thirsty and have to keep coming here to draw water."

16 He told her, "Go, call your husband and come back."

17 "I have no husband," she replied.

Jesus said to her, "You are right when you say you have no husband.

18 The fact is, you have had five husbands, and the man you now have is not your husband. What you have just said is quite true."

19 "Sir," the woman said, "I can see that you are a prophet.

20 Our ancestors worshiped on this mountain, but you Jews claim that the place where we must worship is in Jerusalem."

21 "Woman," Jesus replied, "believe me, a time is coming when you will worship the Father neither on this mountain nor in Jerusalem.

Many stories about Jesus have their roots in the Old Testament. The gospels were written to explain to the Jews and gentiles of those times that Jesus was the Savior; the long awaited one, whose coming was predicted by the prophets. That's why the authors continuously refer to the Scriptures, and why the symbolism of their stories so often have parallels in the Old Testament.

Jacob and Rachel at the well

The much discussed encounter of Jesus with the unnamed Samaritan woman takes place at the well of the Jewish patriarch Jacob, says verse 6. By specifying this well the author aims to convey the underlying theme of this story. Let's therefore first have a look at the Book of Genesis, where Jacob sees his future wife for the first time at the well where she watered her flocks (see pages 48 and 50).

This story is about the necessity of the sublimation of our lower nature in order for the sacred marriage to take place. Our animalistic forces must be purified and we must gain mastery over them.

A series of clear indications help us to properly interpret this story: The name *Rachel* means "ewe" (female sheep). She is the daughter of *Laban*, which means "white" (pure), and she is a *shepherd* (verse 9), which demonstrates that she is master over the bestial.

In verse 10, Jacob removes the stone from the mouth of the well and lets the sheep drink. A well, being a deep water shaft in the earth, is a perfect metaphor for the spinal column with the kundalini-energy flowing through it. The *sushumna-nadi*, which runs through the spinal column, is energetically closed off at the bottom in the pelvis, to prevent a premature awakening of the kundalini. This is the stone which seals the well. Jacob removes it and lets the animal forces drink from the kundalini-well. Subsequently, these forces are purified.

Immediately after this he kisses Rachel – a woman who he has never seen before! – and begins to weep (verse 11). The kiss refers to the inner merging of the masculine and feminine: the sacred marriage. The weeping refers to the production of *amrita* in the brain.

22 You Samaritans worship what you do not know; we worship what we do know, for salvation is from the Jews.

23 Yet a time is coming and has now come when the true worshipers will worship the Father in the Spirit and in truth, for they are the kind of worshipers the Father seeks.

24 God is spirit, and his worshipers must worship in the Spirit and in truth."

25 The woman said, "I know that Messiah" (called Christ) "is coming. When he comes, he will explain everything to us."

26 Then Jesus declared, "I, the one speaking to you—I am he."

The Disciples Rejoin Jesus

27 Just then his disciples returned and were surprised to find him talking with a woman. But no one asked, "What do you want?" or "Why are you talking with her?"

28 Then, leaving her water jar, the woman went back to the town and said to the people,

29 "Come, see a man who told me everything I ever did. Could this be the Messiah?"

30 They came out of the town and made their way toward him.

31 Meanwhile his disciples urged him, "Rabbi, eat something."

32 But he said to them, "I have food to eat that you know nothing about."

33 Then his disciples said to each other, "Could someone have brought him food?"

34 "My food," said Jesus, "is to do the will of him who sent me and to finish his work.

(John 4:1-34)

Jacob Arrives in Paddan Aram

1 Then Jacob continued on his journey and came to the land of the eastern peoples.

2 There he saw a well in the open country, with three flocks of sheep lying near it because the flocks were watered from that well. The stone over the mouth of the well was large.

3 When all the flocks were gathered there, the shepherds would roll the stone away from the well's mouth and water the sheep. Then they would return the stone to its place over the mouth of the well.

4 Jacob asked the shepherds, "My brothers, where are you from?"

"We're from Harran," they replied.

5 He said to them, "Do you know Laban, Nahor's grandson?"

"Yes, we know him," they answered.

6 Then Jacob asked them, "Is he well?"

"Yes, he is," they said, "and here comes his daughter Rachel with the sheep."

7 "Look," he said, "the sun is still high; it is not time for the flocks to be gathered. Water the sheep and take them back to pasture."

The fact that Rachel and Jacob are family (they are cousins), is in the language of symbolism a way of telling us that the story relates of a spiritual process *within* Jacob.

The Samaritan woman

The encounter of Jesus with the Samaritan woman revolves around the same theme as the encounter of Jacob with Rachel. This woman has no animals with her but she is a gentile which in the Bible is also a symbol for the lower nature. The town where this story plays is called Sychar (verse 5), and that name means "drunk"; a reference to spiritual unawareness.

Jesus personifies the Divine, and when he takes place *atop* the well (the Greek word *epi* means "on", verse 6) he emphasizes the well as metaphor for the spinal column, with the kundalini-energy flowing within.

It was about the sixth hour, says the source text of verse 6, which refers to the sixth chakra, the place where the sacred marriage takes place. The sixth hour is noon on our time scale; the hottest time of the day. Getting water at that time was highly unusual. Women did this in the morning, or just before sunset when it was cooler. This incongruity emphasizes the symbolism of this number.

Jacob kissed Rachel but the evangelist could of course not let the Son of God kiss this heathen woman. The decorum of those days wouldn't even let him simply talk with her; which explains the reaction of the disciples in verse 27.

The sacred marriage is therefore suggested in a different and more subtle way. *"Go, call your husband and come back,"* says Jesus to the woman in verse 16. When the woman submits that she has no husband his answer is: *"you have had five husbands, and the man you have now is not your husband"* (verse 18). The suspiciously generous number of five husbands, which the woman was supposed to have had, refers to the five senses to which she was "married." The lower nature feeds itself with the stimuli of the senses. With the sixth man she is not yet married: the sacred marriage has not yet taken place.

Living water, mentioned by Jesus in verse 10, refers to the kundalini-energy.

8 "We can't," they replied, "until all the flocks are gathered and the stone has been rolled away from the mouth of the well. Then we will water the sheep."

9 While he was still talking with them, Rachel came with her father's sheep, for she was a shepherd.

10 When Jacob saw Rachel daughter of his uncle Laban, and Laban's sheep, he went over and rolled the stone away from the mouth of the well and watered his uncle's sheep.

11 Then Jacob kissed Rachel and began to weep aloud.

(Gen 29:1-11)

To receive this living water we must be prepared to let go of the body (the senses) and the world. That is the deeper meaning of the water jar which the woman leaves behind in verse 28, and the people who leave the city in order to go to Jesus (God) in verse 30.

This story too contains a reference to *amrita*, namely in verse 32. Jesus doesn't burst out into tears, as Jacob did, but he does evoke the consternation of his disciples when he doesn't eat anything. His enigmatic answer is: *"I have food to eat that you know nothing about."* Whoever conquers his lower nature and the world, as he did, will be fed by God with *amrita*. Amrita is called *manna* in the Bible, and in the next chapter we will have a closer look at this miraculous heavenly bread.

> *To him who overcomes, I will give some of the hidden manna...*
> (Rev 2:17)

The kind of worshipers the Father seeks....
This story also contains an extraordinary plea of Jesus for the internal path. It's one of those remarkable texts in the Bible that become a true joy when understood.

Central to our story is the living water that yields eternal life. We attain eternal life through an immortal light body, or body of resurrection, that is formed during the process of kundalini awakening. Jesus, as representative of God on earth, wants to give us this living water, and this will be in us a *spring of water that wells up* ... (verse 14), a beautiful image of the divine energy that awakens and ascends through the spinal column.

A discussion erupts between Jesus and the woman about the proper place of worship. Until a century earlier the Samaritans had a temple on Mount Gerizim. It had been destroyed but Mount Gerizim remained to the Samaritans a place of worship (verse 20). To the Jews the temple in Jerusalem was the central place at which God was worshipped. Jesus says, *"Woman, believe me, a time is coming when you will worship the Father neither on this mountain nor in Jerusalem."* A shocking statement! No bickering about which place is the proper one: neither are what God wants!

51

Jesus elucidates this in verse 23: "... *true worshipers will worship the Father in the Spirit and in truth...*" The Greek word for spirit, *pneuma*, is also used for the Holy Spirit in the gospels. The Holy Spirit is the Biblical term for the kundalini-shakti.

Then follows perhaps the most important statement of the entire Bible: "*... for they are the kind of worshipers the Father seeks.*"

The Father does not seek the one who visits temples and complies with codes of conduct, but the one who makes of him- or herself a temple for God to dwell in. This person is not directed by sensual pleasures, but abandons his or her water jar and the city to search for Him. By this person He lets Himself be found.

In verse 10, Jesus calls the kundalini the gift of God: "*If you knew the gift of God ..., you would have asked him and he would have given you living water.*"
The holy energy in our pelvis is a gift from God. It's not meant to whimsically experiment with or to put in service of our ego. When we ask, says Jesus, God will give it to us. He will roll the stone away from the well and quench our thirst for all eternity.

> *Ask and it will be given to you; seek and you will find; knock and the door will be opened to you.*
> *For everyone who asks receives; the one who seeks finds; and to the one who knocks, the door will be opened.*
> (Matt 7:7-8)

The John-Jesus-transformation and the sacred marriage

In many places in the Bible we find symbolism that refers to the sacred marriage. Also in the transformation of John into Jesus we see examples of this.

The friend of the Groom

In the gospel of John, Jesus and John the Baptist appear for a short while simultaneously until John exits the stage due to his imprisonment. John's disciples see Jesus as a competing baptist, and interview John about this. John subsequently adds a few deep and wise statements about how matters relate:

26 *They came to John and said to him, "Rabbi, that man who was with you on the other side of the Jordan—the one you testified about—look, he is baptizing, and everyone is going to him."*

27 *To this John replied, "A person can receive only what is given them from heaven.*

28 *You yourselves can testify that I said, 'I am not the Messiah but am sent ahead of him.'*

29 **The bride belongs to the bridegroom. The friend who attends the bridegroom waits and listens for him, and is full of joy when he hears the bridegroom's voice.** *That joy is mine, and it is now complete.*

30 *He must become greater; I must become less."*
(John 3:26-30)

When John says that he has to become less and Jesus more (verse 30), he means: his ego must disappear and make way for the Christ. He calls himself *the friend who attends the bridegroom and waits and listens for him* (verse 29); an image that tells us that John is a witness of the sacred marriage that takes place within him – a mystical process that bypasses the ego, but of which the joy fills the entire person, including the dissipating ego. The author deliberately uses the word "complete" to describe John's joy (verse 29), which refers to the completion of the spiritual process in which John disappears and Jesus is "born."

After the words *"He must become greater; I must become less"* (verse 30) John continues with a mystical discourse that is generally regarded as an expression of praise for Jesus, but in fact Jesus' name is mentioned nowhere. All bias aside, these words could just as well be about John.

The one who comes from above is above all; the one who is from the earth belongs to the earth, and speaks as one from the earth. The one who comes from heaven is above all.
He testifies to what he has seen and heard, but no one accepts his testimony.

Whoever has accepted it has certified that God is truthful.
For the one whom God has sent speaks the words of God, for God gives the
Spirit without limit.
The Father loves the Son and has placed everything in his hands.
Whoever believes in the Son has eternal life, but whoever rejects the Son will
not see life, for God's wrath remains on them.
(John 3:31-36)

John was sent by God, but his testimony is accepted by nobody. The *Son* is
the Christ who has taken up permanent residence within him.

Mary and Joseph

The second example of a Biblical reference to the sacred marriage occurs in
the gospel of Luke. De annunciation of the birth of Jesus begins with the
following two verses:

> 26 *In the sixth month of Elizabeth's pregnancy, God sent the angel Gabriel to*
>   *Nazareth, a town in Galilee,*
> 27 *to a virgin pledged to be married to a man named Joseph, a descendant of*
>   *David. The virgin's name was Mary.*
>   (Luke 1:26-27)

The opening statement of a Biblical story often contains important information about the deeper content of the text that follows. This story opens
with informing the reader that in Elizabeth's sixth month Gabriel was sent
to Mary. Then follows the notion of an imminent marriage: that between
Mary and Joseph (verse 27). The "sixth month" relates to the sixth chakra;
that place within a person where the sacred marriage, the merger between
masculine and feminine energies, takes place.

In this context, Mary symbolizes the internal bride (the *ida-nadi*) of the
sacred marriage, and Joseph, her fiancé, refers to the groom (the *pingala-nadi*). After their unification at the level of the sixth chakra of John – as will
become clear in the following paragraph: it's to him that this passage refers
– the Christ-child will be born in his heart.

Kundalini-awakening

The account of Joseph, Mary and the infant Jesus essentially discusses an internal human process. This is made clear in the text that follows. After the famous annunciation of Jesus' birth, Mary goes to visit her cousin Elizabeth, who is pregnant with John.

> 39 *And Mary arose in these days and went into the hill country with haste, into a city of Judah;*
> 40 *and entered into the house of Zacharias and saluted Elisabeth.*
> 41 *And it came to pass, when Elisabeth heard the salutation of Mary, the babe leaped in her womb; and Elisabeth was filled with the Holy Spirit;*
> 42 *and she lifted up her voice with a loud cry, and said, Blessed art thou among women, and blessed is the fruit of thy womb.*
> 43 *And whence is this to me, that the mother of my Lord should come unto me?*
> 44 *For behold, when the voice of thy salutation came into mine ears, the babe leaped in my womb for joy.*
> 45 *And blessed is she that believed; for there shall be a fulfilment of the things which have been spoken to her from the Lord.*
> (Luke 1:39-45, ASV)

Mary now represents the kundalini-energy, or Holy Spirit, which awakens in the pelvis of Elizabeth and ascends toward the crown chakra. Hence Mary "arose" (in Greek: *anistemi*, to stand up) and hurried to the "hill country" (verse 39), and *"Elizabeth was filled with the Holy Spirit"* (verse 41).
In verse 43 Elizabeth exclaims, " *... whence is this to me, that the mother of my Lord* (i.e. the kundalini, "God the Mother") *should come unto me?"*

Despite what popular translations may suggest, the text never explicitly mentions a *child* of Mary (the word used in verse 42 is *karpos*, meaning fruit). Only Elizabeth's child is mentioned (using the word *brephos*, or babe).

In verse 42, Elizabeth blesses the "fruit of the womb" of Mary. The Greek word *koilia*, which is translated here as womb, literally means "belly." Also the "fruit of the belly" is a covert reference to the kundalini-energy. Jesus uses this same word *koilia* in his metaphor of living water that would flow from our belly:

Whoever believes in me, as Scripture has said, rivers of living water will flow from within [koilia] them." By this he meant the Spirit, whom those who believed in him were later to receive ...
(John 7:38-39)

An important aspect of the meeting between the two women is that via Elizabeth, John too is infused with the Holy Spirit, as was foretold by the angel Gabriel. It is after all *his* spiritual development which is central to the first chapter of Luke. That's why verse 40 opens by stating that Mary entered the *house of Zechariah*. The Greek word for house – *oikos* – not only means "house" as in four walls and a roof, but also refers to genealogy and family.

Our story reveals that John experiences a complete kundalini-awakening. We read in verse 41 that John leaps for joy within Elizabeth's womb, upon hearing Mary's salute. In verse 44 we read the same thing, but now the ears of Elizabeth are explicitly mentioned: *when the voice of thy salutation came into mine ears ...*

In other words: when the kundalini ascended from the pelvis and arrived at the ears (that is: the head, where the completion of the kundalini-transformation-process occurs) John leapt for joy. The Greek word *agalliasis*, which here is translated with "joy" means more than that. It reflects intense and blissful exultation. At the completion of the kundalini-process, John experiences the ecstasy of the mystic.

Verse 45 uses the Greek word *teleiosis*, which means completion or fulfillment. The spiritual completion of John, however, probably did not take place in the womb. It's a Lucan device – as is the note that his mother Elizabeth was in fact barren – to tell us that John, although a man of flesh and blood, was a very special man, with a very special destiny.

The Holy Spirit in our spinal column

All four gospels tell that when Jesus is baptized in the Jordan River, the Spirit of God descends on him.

And Jesus, when He had been baptized, went up straightway out of the water. And lo, the heavens were opened unto Him, and He saw the Spirit of God descending like a dove and lighting upon Him.
(Matt 3:16, KJ21)

The Spirit of God who descends on Jesus, is the kundalini that awakens in John. His arising out of the water describes the ascent of the divine energy in the spinal column (water is a recurring symbol in the Bible for the kundalini). The "heavens that were opened", is the crown chakra of John, which is fully opened to let the light of God flow in. The purifying energy transforms his consciousness, and John is reborn as Jesus, the awakened person. This small scene tells of a process that in reality takes years to complete.

After his awakening, John – now named Jesus in the gospels – proceeds to baptize others with this transcendental kundalini-fire.

11 *"I baptize you with water for repentance. But after me comes one who is more powerful than I, whose sandals I am not worthy to carry. He will baptize you with the Holy Spirit and fire.*
12 *His winnowing fork is in his hand, and he will clear his threshing floor, gathering his wheat into the barn and burning up the chaff with unquenchable fire."*
(Matt 3:11-12)

With a winnowing fork (verse 12), chaff was separated from grain. It was a wooden fork with which the threshed grain was tossed up in the air. The heavier grain fell back down to earth but the chaff was carried away by the wind. This winnowing fork represents the spinal column through which the purifying, *unquenchable fire* of the kundalini flows.

In John's gospel John the Baptist says it slightly differently:

26 *John answered them, saying, I baptize in water: in the midst of you standeth one whom ye know not,*
27 *even he that cometh after me, the latchet of whose shoe I am not worthy to unloose.*
(John 1:26-27, ASV)

The Holy Family, by Gaetano Gandolfi, circa 1775.
Private collection.

Joseph's staff sprouts, which is a symbol for the spinal column in which the awakened kundalini flows. *"The staff belonging to the man I choose will sprout"* (Num 17:5). Mary subtly bares the back of Jesus and Josephs points at him.

At the time at which John tells the Pharisees, *"in the midst of you standeth one whom ye know not,"* Jesus was nowhere near as he enters the scene only the next day (John 1:29). *"In the midst of you"* refers to the kundalini in the spinal column, which the Pharisees do not know.

John baptized in Aenon

The evangelist John has left an extra clue in his gospel for us to unravel the identity of Jesus, by mentioning two mysterious place names where John the Baptist supposedly baptized:

> *After this, Jesus and his disciples went out into the Judean countryside, where he spent some time with them, and baptized.* **Now John also was baptizing at Aenon near Salim,** *because there was plenty of water, and people were coming and being baptized.*
> (John 3:22-23)

Bible researchers have been unable to establish where either Aenon or Salim may have been located, and this may indicate that the author has made these names up in order to convey a message. The name Aenon is most probably a transliteration of the Semitic 'ayin, meaning well.

In the next chapter of this gospel the author proceeds with the story of Jesus and the Samaritan woman at the well. As we saw earlier, the well is in this story a metaphor for the spinal column and the kundalini-energy that runs through it.

The name Salim is related to the familiar Hebrew word *shalom*, meaning peace in the sense of wholeness or unbrokenness; two aspects which a person experiences upon a kundalini-awakening: a great inner peace and wholeness.

By mentioning Aenon en Salim the evangelist wants to convey to us that John not only baptized with water he also baptized with the Holy Spirit (after his transformation to Jesus).

The goddess Shakti, here in the emanation of Durga on a thangka
(a Tibetan Buddhist painting on cotton).

The decapitation of John

Concerning the fate of John the Baptist the gospel of John merely tells that Herod imprisoned him (John 3:24). The synoptics – Matthew, Mark and Luke – write that Herod has John decapitated while in prison. Decapitation is a universal metaphor for the death of the ego.

The decapitation of John is a symbolic reference to spiritual awakening. In the gospels of Matthew and Mark this is made evident by the event that precedes his execution.

6 *But when Herod's birthday came, the daughter of Herodias danced in the midst, and pleased Herod.*

7 *Whereupon he promised with an oath to give her whatsoever she should ask.*

8 *And she, being put forward by her mother, saith, Give me here on a platter the head of John the Baptist.*
   (Matt 14:6-8, ASV; also see Mark 6:21-24)

The dance of Herod's daughter represents kundalini-activity. Dancing is a common metaphor for the working of this energy; an example of this is the wild, ecstatic dance of the mother-goddess Kali from Hinduism. Kali expresses the purifying aspect of the kundalini, and traditionally she is depicted wearing a string of bloody, chopped-off heads for a necklace; trophies of all the egos she has destroyed with the exuberant and ruthless motions of her gyrating arms and legs. In her milder form she is Durga, the warrior-goddess. With her serene exterior Durga too wields the sword for our benefit.

The evangelists knew very well that Herod's daughter was named Salome. Still, her name is consistently left out. Both Matthew and Mark speak merely of the "daughter of Herodias," indicating that this story is not about the historical person Salome, but about the kundalini-energy, the feminine aspect of God.

Verse 6 states that the daughter of Herodias *dances in their midst* (in Greek: *mesos*), which refers to the spinal column. She does this on the birthday

The death of John the Baptist, fresco, circa 1200.
Church of St. John the Baptist, Müstair, Switzerland.

of Herod. The birth which in this case is celebrated is that of the new man (Jesus), made possible by the decapitation of the old man (John); the rebirth which is required to enter the Kingdom of God (John 3:3).

The dance of the kundalini can be painful and cause havoc when not properly guided, but it can also be sensual and yield experiences of bliss. Herod is so moved by the dancing of the daughter of Herodias that he is willing to give her whatever she would ask of him (verse 7). Someone who has experienced any aspect of the Divine is often willing to surrender everything else. The gospel of Matthew deliberately illustrates this:

> The kingdom of heaven is like treasure hidden in a field. When a man found it, he hid it again, and then in his joy went and sold all he had and bought that field.
> Again, the kingdom of heaven is like a merchant looking for fine pearls.
> When he found one of great value, he went away and sold everything he had and bought it.
> (Matt 13:44-46)

Incited by her mother, the girl asks Herod for the head of John. The dance of the kundalini ultimately results in a spiritual decapitation, or death of the ego. John is reborn as Jesus. This new man possesses special powers and gifts. The synoptics (Matthew, Mark and Luke) point toward this rebirth in the form of the curious reaction of Herod, when he hears the miraculous stories about Jesus:

> King Herod heard about this, for Jesus' name had become well known. Some were saying, "John the Baptist has been raised from the dead, and that is why miraculous powers are at work in him."
> Others said, "He is Elijah."
> And still others claimed, "He is a prophet, like one of the prophets of long ago."
> But when Herod heard this, he said, "John, whom I beheaded, has been raised from the dead!"
> (Mark 6:14-16; also see Matthew 14:1-2 and Luke 9:7)

"Jesus is John raised from the dead!" Herod exclaims with amazing certi-

The decapitation of John the Baptist, by Pierre Cécile Puvis de Chavannes, ca 1869.
The National Gallery, London.

tude, as if resurrections like this happened all the time in Judea. And this is precisely what happened in the spiritual sense: John was raised from the spiritual death. He renounced his ego and the name that went with it. With new powers and a new name, rooted in God, he now continues on his way.

Two remarkable paintings

I have found two remarkable and fascinating paintings of the beheading of John, in which the artist refers to the kundalini-proces. The first one is an early 13th century fresco of the Church of St. John the Baptist in Müstair, Switzerland (see page 62). The pattern of Salome's dress resembles the skin of a snake. By having her dance upside down, with two strands of hair flowing upward into one strand, to the top of the head, the kundalini-symbolism is reinforced. The black color of her dress refers to the 'black bride', one of the epithets of the kundalini-goddess. The snake motif returns in the instruments of the two musicians.

The sarcophagus in which John is buried is covered with a black cloth with a pattern that resembles the one of Salome's dress. John's head is not displayed on a platter, as usual and in accordance with the gospels (Mark 6:28 and Matthew 14:11), but has been put in a cup. This is a reference to what later traditions would describe with the legend of the holy grail: the "cup" containing *amrita*, the elixir of immortality.

Perhaps the most remarkable feature of this fresco is its central placing above the altar and a crucifix, which rather strangely results in John's decapitated head hovering just over the crucified Jesus. This, however, completely corresponds with our interpretation that these two events, basically, relate of the death of the same person. And both events, on a metaphorical level, express the death of the ego in the gospels.

The second painting is *The decapitation of John the Baptist*, by the prominent 19th century French painter Pierre Cécile Puvis de Chavannes (see page 64). We see John kneeling, full of resignation and surrender, just before he is decapitated. To his left stand Herodias, her daughter Salome and Herod (or is it a servant?), holding on to the platter upon which the head of John will shortly be placed.

Fig tree leaf

Puvis de Chavannes also connects the execution of John to the crucifixion of Jesus, and uses obvious kundalini-symbolism. Directly behind John stands a fig tree; the tree which in spiritual traditions is the quintessential symbol of the spinal column and the energies that flow through it.

One of the typical leaves of the fig tree lies rather conspicuously on the ground next to John. This leaf deliberately draws our attention to the tree behind John. With it the artist states that John's decapitation is the consequence of the working of the kundalini-energy.

Central to the composition is the cross that John holds in his hand. The presence of this radiating cross connects in no uncertain terms the decapitation of John with the Jesus' crucifixion. It is clear that the artist aims to convey in imagery what I have tried to convey in words.

It's intriguing that this painting appears to be unfinished, while it was nevertheless in the possession of Puvis de Chavannes for about thirty years. The three figures on the right of the painting don't have the detailed pronunciation of John and his executioner and lack depth because of that. Did the artist thus suggest that these three people – Herod, Herodias and Salome – are fictional characters in a myth which in essence relates of an inner process of rebirth?

This fascinating painting can't be forgotten once one's eyes have rested on it. It was produced around 1869 and remained the property of Puvis de Chavannes until his death in 1898 – a work of art that evidently also clung to its creator.

3

The name Jesus
and the fish as symbol

I have heard your prayer and seen your tears; I will heal you. On the third day from now you will go up to the temple of the Lord.

2 Kings 20:5

The angel who visits Mary and announces the birth of her son instructs her to give him the name Jesus (Luke 1:31). Why Jesus? In this chapter we will unravel the deeper meaning of this name. We will find surprising connections with Joshua and Jonah from the Old Testament, and we will discover how the Ichtus (fish) has become a symbol of Jesus. Solving this mystery will also reveal why the enigmatic prophetess Anna from the New Testament never leaves the temple, and how the apostle Paul overcame his blindness.

The name Jesus

The name Jesus is the Greek version of the Hebrew name Joshua. Naming someone Jesus in those days meant naming him after the man who led Israel across the Jordan and into the Promised Land: Joshua the son of Nun

The name Joshua – or more fully: Yahu-shua' – means "YHWH saves". It consists of two elements:

The first part is the shortened version of the name of God: Yahweh.
1) The second part comes from the verb *yasha'*, which means to save or deliver.

The central letter of this verb *yasha is* also the most pronounced one: the letter *shin*:

Ancient Hebrew   Modern Hebrew

The Hebrew alphabet developed from pictograms, and letters weren't simply abstract symbols but rather little pictures. These pictures had names and meanings, and Hebrew words formed like little comic strips in which every letter had its individual meaning. In that same tradition of having single letters represent whole concepts, the letter *shin* came to represent God's name Shaddai. Until today, Jewish priests form this letter with their hands when they pronounce the Priestly Blessing.

Detail of a mozaic in the Synagoge of Enschede (the Netherlands).

This letter *shin* is written as a horizontal line with on it three vertical lines. It is a character that resembles a trident (a large fork with three prongs), which is an attribute that frequently appears in religious iconography. For example the Greek god Poseidon – or Neptune to the Romans – is inseparable from the trident. But also the Hindu deities Shiva and Ganesha are often depicted with a so-called trishula. This universal "trident of salvation" is a reference to the three energy channels: ida, sushumna and pingala, and by extension to a kundalini-awakening.

Fittingly, the term *Shekinah* – the Judaic equivalent of the kundalini – starts with a *shin*. And it is no coincidence that, just as the spine is located in the middle of the body, we find the *shin* in the middle of the name Joshua. Which, interestingly, is also the case with the Hebrew word *Mashiah* (Messiah; anointed one).

To find out what the exact nature is of the salvation implied in the name "YHWH saves", we have to back to the book Exodus, to the first Jesus in the Old Testament: Joshua the son of Nun, Israel's national hero.

Joshua, the successor of Moses

The name Jesus/Joshua was in Biblical times one of the most frequently occurring Jewish names, and one of more than a dozen names derived from our verb *yasha* (Hosea, Isaiah, even the familiar phrase Hosanna all come from this verb). There are four men named Joshua mentioned in the Old

Testament. The first and most famous Joshua received his name from Moses himself (his original name was Hosea, meaning "salvation"; Num 13:8 and 16). This Joshua would become the successor of Moses and lead the people of Israel to the land Canaan, promised to them by God.

The Promised Land is a metaphor for a state of consciousness in which the individual experiences a (renewed) living connection with God[4]. Jesus calls this state of consciousness the Kingdom of God. The individual returns to the Paradise from which Adam and Eve were expelled.

The Jesus-John transformation is parallel to the Moses-Joshua account. Both John and Moses represent the old man who goes on a quest for the Kingdom of God (the Promised Land). This old man will first have to die (i.e. the ego must die), before a unification with God can take place.

Moses dies, therefore, just before the Israelites would enter the Promised Land. But God shows it to him, from afar:

> [4] *Then the Lord said to him, "This is the land I promised on oath to Abraham, Isaac and Jacob when I said, 'I will give it to your descendants.' I have let you see it with your eyes, but you will not cross over into it."*
> [5] *And Moses the servant of the Lord died there in Moab, as the Lord had said.*
> [6] *He buried him in Moab, in the valley opposite Beth Peor, but to this day no one knows where his grave is.*
> (Deut 34:4-6)

If this were an account of what actually happened, it seems unjust and painful. After forty years of trudging through the desert and faithfulness to God, Moses is granted a glimpse of the Promised Land but is not allowed to *cross over into it* (verse 4). We may, however, regard these events as metaphor for spiritual growth, and then the story of Moses becomes hopeful and inspiring.

Just before his death, Moses hands the leadership over to Joshua by means of the laying on of hands:

71

Now Joshua son of Nun was filled with the spirit of wisdom because Moses had laid his hands on him. So the Israelites listened to him and did what the Lord had commanded Moses.
(Deut 34:9)

The *spirit of wisdom* with which Joshua was hence filled, is the kundalini, which Moses, via the laying on of his hands, caused to awaken in him. Here we see a beautiful parallel with the gospels, in which the Holy Spirit descends on Jesus upon his baptism by John.

Understanding the gospels
Seeing the similarities between the two stories is crucial for understanding the deeper message of the gospels. The transition from John (old man) to Jesus (new man) follows the same basic pattern as the transition between Moses and his successor Joshua. Like John, Moses is a prophet whose life plays out in the desert, until he definitely exits the stage and is replaced by Jesus/Joshua, whose name represents a man born-again in God. The moment of transition is marked by a kundalini-awakening.

The first thing the Joshua of the Old Testament does when Moses has passed away and he has become leader of Israel, is to cross the river Jordan into the Promised Land. In the gospels too we find references to Jesus being on the side of the Jordan other than the one where John was active (John 1:28 and 3:26).

The Jordan represents in the Bible the *sushumna-nadi*, the energy channel in the spinal column[5]. "Crossing the Jordan" is a transformation metaphor that refers to a kundalini-awakening.

Joshua, son of Nun
The successor of Moses, as we saw above in the quote from the Book of Deuteronomy, is called *Joshua, son of Nun*, and the addition "son of Nun" has held for many centuries a well kept mystical secret.
Nun is both a Semitic word meaning "fish" and a Hebrew letter (נ).

Ancient Hebrew had no special characters for numbers, but the regular Hebrew characters had been assigned numerical values. Our letter *nun* rep-

72

resented the number 50. That means that the numerical equivalent of the term "son of Nun" is "son of Fifty".

In the time in which fingers were used to calculate, the number ten (all fingers) represented "fullness". The number five (one hand) therefore represented "half."

Charged with this subliminal symbolism from antiquity, the number five went on to assume a very special role in the Bible stories. Five (or fifty or five hundred) often points to the higher or lower nature of a human being.

The addition to Joshua's name – the son of Fifty – indicates that he lived out of his higher nature; he is a "son of God." In numerology zeroes are commonly disregarded and the number five has in principle the same symbolic value as fifty. It might still be possible, however, that in this case fifty has extra meaning. Fifty is five times ten: the higher nature (five) brought to fullness (ten)?

The ten commandments of Moses

Possibly the most graceful instance of the symbolism of five is in the Ten Commandments, which Moses received from God in the Book of Exodus. These behavioral rules, written by God on two stone tablets, reflect the dual nature of man. The first five commands refer to our higher nature, and the second five are clearly meant to bridle our lower, animal nature.

The Ten Commandments – abridged and organized according to the Jewish tradition:
1. I am the Lord your God, who brought you out of Egypt, out of the land of slavery.
2. You shall have no other gods before me.
3. You shall not misuse the name of the Lord your God, for the Lord will not hold anyone guiltless who misuses his name.
4. Remember the Sabbath day by keeping it holy.
5. Honor your father and your mother, so that you may live long in the land the Lord your God is giving you.
6. You shall not murder.
7. You shall not commit adultery.

Moses receives the Ten Commandments on two tables from God

8. You shall not steal.
9. You shall not give false testimony against your neighbor.
10. You shall not covet anything that belongs to your neighbor.

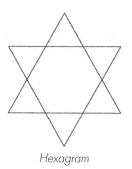

Hexagram

These two clusters of five commandments each also correspond to the two triangles of the hexagram. This six-pointed star is an ancient symbol which is found in many spiritual traditions. It expresses the merger of opposites – including our higher and lower nature. The hexagram appears in the Old Testament as the "star of David"[6] or the "seal of Solomon"

The hexagram is often associated with the heart, which is energetically the place in a person where the higher and lower forces (chakras) meet, and where the Divine settles after the integration of either halves has taken place.

The Ichthus

The Ichthus

As stated above, *nun* is also a regular Semitic word, which means "fish". Joshua, therefore, is called "son of Fish." The fish as symbol for Jesus arose in early Christianity. Several popular theories have tried to explain this so-called Ichthus (after *ikhthýs*, the Greek word for "fish") but scholars are far from consensus. I think that the symbol of the fish refers to the kundalini-awakening of Jesus, drawing on the esoteric meaning of the name of his predecessor Joshua the son of Nun (Fish).

The vesica piscis

The shape of the Christian Ichthus was derived from the *vesica piscis*: the ancient ge-

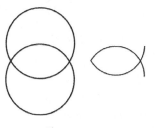

The vesica piscis

75

ometric form in which two partly overlapping circles yield two stylized fish. It's a symbol that represents – just like the hexagram – the merger of opposites: the sacred marriage.

Jonah and the Great Fish

A typical example from the Old Testament in which the deeper meaning of *nun* takes a central place is the familiar story of Jonah and the Great Fish. Popular folklore usually has a whale gobbling up Jonah, but that's not what the text says:

> Now the Lord had prepared a great fish to swallow up Jonah. And Jonah was in the belly of the fish three days and three nights.
> (Jonah 1:17, KJ21)

Briefly summarized, this story is about a recalcitrant prophet who, after a three day stay in the belly of a great fish (metaphor for the kundalini process) is spewed out onto the shore (a metaphor for connecting to the Divine). Subsequently God commands him to save the population of Nineveh (a contraction of *nun* and YHWH) from their demise (spiritual unconsciousness).

In the Bible, three days represent a period of transformation and renewal. The most familiar event that happened "after three days" is the resurrection of Jesus from the grave. Shortly, we will also have a look at the example of Paul who was blind for three days.
This period of three days, which is required for transformation, coincides with the waxing of the moon: the new moon which re-appears every time after a period of three days of darkness.

Jonah is cast out of the ship

The Book of Jonah is from beginning to end about the process of kundalini awakening. Let's have a look at the main events. During a heavy storm Jonah is cast overboard by his ship mates. The sea is a universal symbol for the subconscious of man. This picture is supposed to tell us that Jonah is being submerged in his own subconscious. The great fish which swallows him up represents the kundalini process.

From the belly of the great fish, Jonah expresses his gratitude for being res-cued:

2   *and said: "I cried by reason of mine affliction unto the Lord,*
    and He heard me.
    Out of the belly of hell cried I,
    and Thou heardest my voice.

3   *For Thou hadst cast me into the deep,*
    in the midst of the seas,
    and the floods compassed me about;
    all Thy billows and Thy waves
    passed over me.

4   *Then I said, 'I am cast out of Thy sight;*
    yet I will look again toward Thy holy temple.'

5   *The waters compassed me about, even to the soul;*
    the depth closed me round about,
    the weeds were wrapped about my head.

6   *To the roots of the mountains I sank down;*
    the earth beneath barred me in forever.
    But you, Lord my God,
    brought my life up from the pit.
    (Jonah 2:2-5, KJ21 and 2:6, NIV)

Poetic words that mirror the joy of someone who deeply within (in his own belly!) experiences the Hand of God. Verse 2 and 3 reveal to us what Jonah is so grateful for: God listened to Jonah's cry and *that is why* God hurled him into the depths.

It is therefore not so much the rescue by the great fish, but rather the being cast into the sea, for which Jonah thanks God. The plunge into the dark deep is a necessary phase in the process of spiritual awakening, the process that ultimately results in great joy. Via his three day stay in the fish, Jonah will be rescued from *the belly of hell* (verse 2); an ingenious wordplay as it refers to being "tormented" by the passions of the (under)belly. Verse 6 re-fers to the incarnation into matter and being captured in a corporeal body. This is what man is rescued from via the kundalini-process, or the great fish.

Jonah concludes his prayer of thanksgiving with: *Salvation comes from the Lord* (Jonah 2:9).
In Hebrew: *yeshu'atah le'yahweh.*
Contracted this statement forms: Joshua (Jesus)!
It appears to be a magic word because:
The Lord commanded the fish, and it vomited Jonah onto dry land. (Jonah 2:10)

The conversion of Nineveh

When Jonah's feet stand once again on solid ground, he receives the following command from God:

> 2 *"Go to the great city of Nineveh and proclaim to it the message I give you."*
> 3 *Jonah obeyed the word of the Lord and went to Nineveh. Now Nineveh was a very large city; it took three days to go through it.*
> 4 *Jonah began by going a day's journey into the city, proclaiming, "Forty more days and Nineveh will be overthrown."*
> (Jonah 3:2-4)

Here the reader begins to recognize a more detailed picture of the transformation process. The number forty (verse 4) indicates in the Bible a transition period. Forty is the total of four times ten and represents the bringing to perfection (ten) of the four aspects of the individual: body, mind, heart (feeling), and soul.

> 6 *For word came unto the king of Nineveh; and he arose from his throne, and he laid his robe from him, and covered himself with sackcloth and sat in ashes.*
> 7 *And he caused it to be proclaimed and published through Nineveh by the decree of the king and his nobles, saying, "Let neither man nor beast, herd nor flock, taste anything; let them not feed, nor drink water.*
> 8 *But let man and beast be covered with sackcloth and cry mightily unto God. Yea, let them turn every one from his evil way, and from the violence that is in their hands.*
> (Jonah 3:6-8, KJ21)

The king of Nineveh represents the ego, and in the process of awakening this ego relinquishes its dominion over the individual (verse 6). The animal nature (the herds and flocks) receive no more nutrition (verse 7). All external display is put off (sackcloth), and an inner change (turn from evil ways) takes place (verse 8).

> 5 *Jonah had gone out and sat down at a place east of the city. There he made himself a shelter, sat in its shade and waited to see what would happen to the city.*
>
> 6 *Then the Lord God provided a leafy plant and made it grow up over Jonah to give shade for his head to ease his discomfort, and Jonah was very happy about the plant.*
>
> 7 *But at dawn the next day God provided a worm, which chewed the plant so that it withered.*
>
> 8 *When the sun rose, God provided a scorching east wind, and the sun blazed on Jonah's head so that he grew faint. He wanted to die, and said, "It would be better for me to die than to live."*
> (Jonah 4:5-8)

This text is permeated with unmistakable kundalini symbolism: the miraculous plant, the worm, the burning sun, Jonah's desire to die ... A few lines after this passage the Book of Jonah stops abruptly, but we know about the missing happy end through the other stories in the Bible: Nineveh is saved and Jonah will, just like John the Baptist and Moses, die and make way for the new man: Joshua ...

The sign of Jonah

In one of his sermons, Jesus makes a connection between his own future resurrection from the dead and Jonah, the great fish and Nineveh:

> *Then some of the Pharisees and teachers of the law said to him, "Teacher, we want to see a sign from you."*
> *He answered, "A wicked and adulterous generation asks for a sign! But none will be given it except the sign of the prophet Jonah.*
> *For as Jonah was three days and three nights in the belly of a huge fish, so the Son of Man will be three days and three nights in the heart of the earth.*
> *The men of Nineveh will stand up at the judgment with this generation and*

condemn it; for they repented at the preaching of Jonah, and now something greater than Jonah is here.
(Matthew 12:38-41)

Jesus' pending death and resurrection will be on a par with the symbolism of the story of Jonah. At this time Jesus has already laid down the old man John and has gone on as the new man Jesus. Soon he will follow God's command and give this inner process physical reality. The three days which Jesus will spend in the grave symbolize the kundalini-process that leads to inner "resurrection," just like Jonah's three days in the belly of the great fish.

Manna from heaven

A word that almost certainly corresponds with the mystical meaning of *nun* is *manna*, the heavenly bread that the Israelites received from God during their forty year trek through the desert:

Then the Lord said to Moses, "I will rain down bread from heaven for you.
(Exodus 16:4)

... and in the morning there was a layer of dew around the camp. When the dew was gone, thin flakes like frost on the ground appeared on the desert floor. When the Israelites saw it, they said to each other, "What is it?" For they did not know what it was. Moses said to them, "It is the bread the Lord has given you to eat.
(Exodus 16:13-15)

The people of Israel called the bread manna. It was white like coriander seed and tasted like wafers made with honey.
(Exodus 16:31)

The Israelites ate manna forty years, until they came to a land that was settled; they ate manna until they reached the border of Canaan.
(Exodus 16:35)

The word *manna* appears to have been invented by the author of this story,

80

and it is subsequently not clear how it was derived. But it looks like it has to do with the particle of inquisition *man*, meaning "what?" (as used in verse 16:15), which in turn derives from a root *mem-nun-nun*. The prefix *mem* normally expresses agent or instrument, and *mem-nun-nun* means quite literally "from Nun."

The heavenly bread is a result of the kundalini-process. What the Bible calls *manna* is dubbed *amrita* in the far-eastern traditions. Both describe the inner sustenance that a person receives from the transformed brain fluids. *Amrita* tastes like honey, and so does *manna* according to verse 16:31. In the following verse the Israelites receive from God a specific instruction for the distribution of the manna. The Hebrew word *gulgoleth*, which is translated as "man" in the quote below, literally means "skull"!

> *This is the thing which the Lord hath commanded: 'Gather of it every man according to his eating, **an omer for every man**, according to the number of your persons. Take ye every man for those who are in his tents.'"*
> (Exodus 16:16, KJ21)

The name Moses
The letter *mem* has an important significance too. The ancient pictogram for this letter resembles water, and that is probably where the name *mem* is derived from: *mayim*, which means *water*.

Ancient Hebrew

Modern Hebrew

Water is in the Bible one of the most frequently used metaphors for the kundalini-energy. The name Moses is the Greek transliteration of the Hebrew name *Moshe*. This was not a typical Hebrew name and is probably an adaptation of an Egyptian original. But written in Hebrew (*mem-shin-he*) this name closely resembles the Hebrew verb for to extract (from water). It's precisely this verb that the daughter of the Pharaoh uses to explain this name: "Because from the water I *drew* him" (Exodus 2:10). Moses enters the

Moses drawn out of the water

Biblical stage as an infant, was famously placed in a basket and left in the reeds on the banks of the Nile river, only to be found and "drawn out" by the daughter of the Pharaoh.

Also this story is pure symbolism. An extraction from water represents here the activation of the kundalini-energy. The (hollow) reed as symbol for the spinal column can be found both in the Bible and in ancient Egyptian culture. The Nile, as does the Jordan, represents the *sushumna-nadi*, through which the kundalini flows from the pelvis to the crown chakra.

Just like the name Joshua and the word Messiah, the name Moshe has the *shin* in its centre. Together with the initial *mem*, this name, perfectly fits an individual that experiences a kundalini-awakening.

Heaven
The powerful symbolism which results from the combination of the letters *mem* and *shin* can also be found in the Hebrew word *shamayim*, "heaven" – as used in Exodus 16:4: "See, I will let bread rain from *heaven* for you". The origin of this word is also an etymological mystery, but as the place from which *manna* comes raining down, it obviously refers to the kundalini-mystery as much as the name Moses.

> *May God give you heaven's* [shamayim] *dew* ...
> (Gen 27:28)

Amen
On the pictogram level the familiar word *amen* (spelled *aleph-mem-nun*) also bristles with kundalini symbolism.

The *aleph* is the first letter of the Hebrew alphabet. The ancient pictogram of this letter is the head of an ox. Its meaning is *power, strength*. The ancient name for *aleph* is *el*. El is one of the names of God in Judaism. All this points at the *aleph* representing "the power of God".

There is no consensus on the etymology of Amen. Several hypotheses exist.

The ancient pictograms of Amen suggest, however, that this word reflects a call for a kundalini-awakening. In the gospel of Matthew (according to most ancient manuscripts and translations), the Lord's Prayer ends with *amen* (Matt 6:9-13). This is a logical conclusion, after asking God for kundalini-related aspects: the (inner) coming of His Kingdom, the receiving of daily bread (*manna*), forgiveness of sins (*karma*), sublimation of the animal forces (temptation), and deliverance from evil (the lower nature).

Very truly I tell you
Many of Jesus' sayings in the gospels are preceded by *amen*. This is usually translated with "very truly." One of the examples:

> *Very truly (amen, amen) I tell you, the one who believes has eternal life. I am the bread of life.*
> *Your ancestors ate the manna in the wilderness, yet they died.*
> *But here is the bread that comes down from heaven, which anyone may eat and not die.*
> *I am the living bread that came down from heaven. Whoever eats this bread will live forever. This bread is my flesh, which I will give for the life of the world."*
> (John 6:47-51)

In the quote above, Jesus refers to *manna* and calls himself the living bread that came down from heaven; bread that gives eternal life. It's a text which connects and confirms what we have discussed in this chapter about the mystical meanings of *amen*, *manna*, and the name Jesus.

Jesus the Amen
In the Book of Revelation Jesus is called the Amen:

> *These are the words of the Amen, the faithful and true witness, the ruler of God's creation.*
> (Rev 3:14)

And the final words of the Bible are:

84

He who testifies to these things says, "Yes, I am coming soon."
Amen. Come, Lord Jesus.
The grace of the Lord Jesus be with God's people. Amen.
(Rev 22:20-21)

All this urges for a Divine awakening of the kundalini in our pelvis.

The prophetess Anna

A striking New Testament example of the usage of the *nun* as symbol for kundalini-awakening comes with the name Anna. This name is a graceful Greek palindrome that hinges on a double *ne*. In Jerusalem, the aging prophetess Anna confesses the baby Jesus as Savior, when his parents have travelled to the temple to dedicate their firstborn, as per Jewish customs:

> [36] *There was also a prophet, Anna, the daughter of Penuel, of the tribe of Asher. She was very old; she had lived with her husband seven years after her marriage,*
> [37] *and then was a widow until she was eighty-four. She never left the temple but worshiped night and day, fasting and praying.*
> [38] *Coming up to them at that very moment, she gave thanks to God and spoke about the child to all who were looking forward to the redemption of Jerusalem.*
> (Luke 2:36-38)

Anna personifies the kundalini, which is also evident from the curious description of her life. A widow, according to Biblical symbolism, represents someone who does not experience a living relationship with God (verse 37). Eighty-four equals seven times twelve. Twelve is the number of spiritual fullness.

The fact that Anna was a widow until she was eighty-four (verse 37) illustrates that the unification with God takes place after all seven chakras have been wholly 'spiritualized' (purified and activated).

The seven years of co-habitation with her husband refers to the inner merger of the opposites on all chakra-levels, which takes place at the sacred marriage.

The conversion of Saul

He fell to the ground and heard a voice say to him,
"Saul, Saul, why do you persecute me?" (Acts 9:4)

Anna was the daughter of Penuel (Greek: *Phanouel*), says the author (verse 36). *Phanouel* refers to the pineal gland – in Latin the *glandula pinealis* – the gland the size of a kernel of rice in de middle of our head, of which the mystical meaning was known about in the ancient Middle-East. In the Book of Genesis, for instance, patriarch Jacob renames the place where he has an impressive experience of God as Penuel (Gen 32:30).

The tribe of Asher, from which Anna hailed, probably refers to *Asherah*: a pagan mother-goddess which represented the kundalini (just like many other goddesses from various cultures). The prophetess who never left the temple (verse 37) illustrates the kundalini which is active in our body (the temple) day and night. Just like Jesus, Anna represents the Divine in us, which wants to redeem (verse 38) us from our sleeping consciousness and our earthly fetters.

The conversion of Paul
The apostle Paul at first fanatically persecutes Christians, but after a mystical experience he turns his ship around and becomes one of the key-figures in the effort to spread the gospel. His remarkable conversion, too, reverberates with the *nun*.

His initiation story looks like that of Jonah, who stayed in the darkness of the belly of the fish for three days. Paul (then still called Saul), is on his way to Damascus when he sees a heavenly light, falls on the ground and stays blind for three days:

3 *As he neared Damascus on his journey, suddenly a light from heaven flashed around him.*
4 *He fell to the ground and heard a voice say to him, "Saul, Saul, why do you persecute me?"*
5 *"Who are you, Lord?" Saul asked.*
"I am Jesus, whom you are persecuting," he replied.
6 *"Now get up and go into the city, and you will be told what you must do."*
7 *The men traveling with Saul stood there speechless; they heard the sound but did not see anyone.*

<blockquote>
8   *Saul got up from the ground, but when he opened his eyes he could see noth-ing. So they led him by the hand into Damascus.*

9   *For three days he was blind, and did not eat or drink anything.*
(Acts 9:3-9)
</blockquote>

The explicit note that Saul falls to the ground during this vision has signif-icance. In the Bible to "get up" denotes a spiritual awakening. Jesus says in verse 6 to Saul: *"Get up ... !"* With that he receives the command to a spiritual "resurrection."

After he arrives in the city Jesus sends a disciple named Ananias to Saul to heal him:

<blockquote>
Then Ananias went to the house and entered it. Placing his hands on Saul, he said, "Brother Saul, the Lord—Jesus, who appeared to you on the road as you were coming here—has sent me so that you may see again and be filled with the Holy Spirit."
Immediately, something like scales fell from Saul's eyes, and he could see again. He got up and was baptized ...
(Acts 9:17-18)
</blockquote>

Ananias, as the reader has doubtlessly surmised, comes from the same sig-nature double-*nun* root *he-nun-nun* as the name Anna. It's also significant that Saul at that moment is lodging in a house on a street *called Straight Street* (Acts 9:11). This is a reference to the spinal column; imagery that also John the Baptist uses: *Make straight the road for the Lord* (John 1:23).

Ananias lays his hands upon Saul and the latter is healed from his *spiritual* blindness. Filled with the Holy Spirit (i.e. the kundalini) he too continues his way under a new name: Paul.

The descent into hell
As noted before, the period of three days of Jonah in the great fish, Saul's blindness, and Jesus' stay in the grave all symbolize the same period of transformation. But what actually happens in this period? About that the stories reveal as good as nothing. It's in any case a period of great darkness; all three metaphors are clear about that. Neither in the belly of a fish nor

in a grave a scintilla of light penetrates. And a blind person too is devoid of light.

The images and words of all three events additionally reflect a downward motion. Saul falls to the ground, Jonah is cast in the depth of the sea, and Jesus stays "in the heart of the earth" (Matt 12:40). It's not part of the Bible, but according to the Christian creed, during his time in the grave he descents into hell. The Roman Catholic version of the creed is as follows:

The Apostles' Creed

1. *I believe in God, the Father almighty, creator of heaven and earth.*
2. *I believe in Jesus Christ, his only Son, our Lord.*
3. *He was conceived by the power of the Holy Spirit and born of the Virgin Mary.*
4. *He suffered under Pontius Pilate, was crucified, died, and was buried.*
5. **He descended into hell. On the third day he rose again.**
6. *He ascended into heaven and is seated at the right hand of the Father.*
7. *He will come again to judge the living and the dead*
8. *I believe in the Holy Spirit,*
9. *the holy catholic Church, the communion of saints,*
10. *the forgiveness of sins,*
11. *the resurrection of the body,*
12. *and the life everlasting.*
13. *Amen.*

The personal hell

The official dogma of the church dictates that Jesus' descent into hell describes his journey to the realm of the dead to redeem the roaming souls there.

Translated to the internal process of the kundalini-awakening it is a submerging in one's subconscious and a confrontation with all old pain and impurities stored therein; a journey which every spiritual aspirant makes during the phase of purification and healing.

Let me be clear: in reality this is not a journey of three days but of years!

Raised on the third day

The permeation of the kundalini-energy releases unprocessed emotions, and particularly at night this yields horrible nightmares. Suppressed anger, sorrow and dismay break loose and become translated into heart-rending dream imagery. The metaphor of time spent in hell is spot on.

During a period of a number of years the person is wholly turned inside out. It is a troubled time during which he or she must find the way in the figurative darkness, because the light of God is not yet or hardly visible. It's a lonely time too. Just like Jonah, you'll be tossed out of your comfort zone (the ship). The concerns of the world lose their meaning to you but a replacement foundation is still lacking. You set course for God but you barely experience him. Travelling companions, people to support you and to relate to, are usually missing as well.

Countless myths, legends and fairy tales from all over the world tell of this journey. It's the universal heroic epos, in which the main character first loses everything and must overcome many obstacles, before he can ascend the royal throne.

The belly as hell
As we have seen, just prior to his salvation Jonah cried out from *the belly of hell* (Jonah 2:2). Hell, or the "underworld," also refers to the energy of the lower chakras, to our underbelly, where feelings of lust keep the soul from being at peace and away from God. "Burning in hell" is being driven by the desires of de lower nature.

These forces must be confronted. One of the pitfalls on the path to a complete awakening is letting the kundalini-energy fuel the lower chakras, instead of the higher. Rousing the kundalini-serpent from her slumber in the pelvis is relatively easy, but successfully guiding her to the crown chakra is something only a few accomplish.

One comforting thought is that although God (the kundalini) may be the one to throw you into this hell, He also aids you in this quest. When you are about to succumb, His loving presence is always there to encourage you and to guide you.

Salvation

The name Jesus means "YHWH saves". We started this chapter with the question: what is the nature of this salvation?

Jesus' predecessor by name, Joshua the son of Nun, 'saved' the people of Israel, guided by God, from wandering in the desert by leading them to the promised land Canaan. The entry into the promised land is a metaphor for attaining an expanded state of consciousness, as a result of a kundalini awakening. One is liberated ('saved') from the ego and all earthly bondage (the desert).

In Psalm 74 the legendary king David begs God to bring his salvation (*yeshua'*) to the middle of the earth:

> 11 *Why withdrawest thou thy hand, even thy right hand?*
> *pluck it out of thy bosom.*
> 12 *For God is my King of old,*
> *working salvation* [yeshua'] *in the midst of the earth.*
> (Psalm 74:11-12, KJ21)

The "midst of the earth" (verse 12) is a metaphor for the spinal column. The hand of God (verse 11) represents the kundalini-energy. The word translated with "bosom" (verse 11) in fact denotes a hollow or cavity that serves as a receptacle for liquids or waste, or anything that "reclines" and collects at the lowest available place. It denotes the pelvic region, where the kundalini resides.

David pleads God to destroy his enemies. These enemies stand for everything in his own psyche that prevents his soul to unite with God. The New Testament Jesus calls these enemies 'sins', and the divine energy that cleanses us from these sins he calls the Spirit of truth:

> *When the Advocate comes, whom I will send to you from the Father--the Spirit of truth who goes out from the Father--he will testify about me.*
> (John 15:26)

This Spirit of truth will help us in overcoming the world; it will set us free:

Then you will know the truth, and the truth will set you free.
(John 8:32)

This Holy Spirit set Jonah free from the hell of the underbelly and saved the apostle Paul from his blindness. This was the same Spirit that saved John the Baptist. Liberated from all earthly bondage, he continued his life as Jesus and began teaching all who were willing to listen how they too could be saved. He shared his knowledge and wisdom with his followers and baptized with the Holy Spirit.

Salvation is God-realization. It is the final result of a long process of cleansing and healing, guided by the Spirit. In the gospel of Luke Jesus speaks powerful words that provide a perfect summarization of this process:

And there was delivered unto Him the book of the prophet Isaiah. And when He had opened the book, He found the place where it was written:
"The Spirit of the Lord is upon Me, because He hath anointed Me to preach the Gospel to the poor. He hath sent Me to heal the brokenhearted, to preach deliverance to the captives, and recovering of sight to the blind, to set at liberty them that are bruised,
to preach the acceptable year of the Lord."
And He closed the book, and He gave it again to the minister and sat down. And the eyes of all those who were in the synagogue were fastened on Him.
(Luke 4:17-20, KJ21)

The deeper meaning of his opening words *"he hath anointed me to preach the Gospel to the poor"* is easily overlooked, because we know that Jesus was very emphatic towards poor people. But why would he make it a priority to preach the gospel to them specifically? Wouldn't giving them comfort or blessing have been more appropriate?
"Poorness" refers to the size of one's ego. Jesus mentions this virtue explicitly in the first blessing of his Sermon on the Mount: *"Blessed are the poor in spirit, for theirs is the kingdom of heaven."* (Matthew 5:3)

93

Meekness, humbleness and modesty are prerequisites to salvation:

> For the LORD taketh pleasure in his people: he will beautify the meek with salvation.
> (Psalm 149:4, KJV)

> When God arose to judgment, to save all the meek of the earth. Selah.
> (Psalm 76:9, KJV)

The image that Jesus uses to measure the ego is the narrow door:

> Then said one unto him, Lord, are there few that be saved? And he said unto them, "Strive to enter in at the strait gate: for many, I say unto you, will seek to enter in, and shall not be able.
> (Luke 13:23-24)

In summary: the salvation that plays such a central role in the New Testament, and after which both Joshua and Jesus were named, refers to man's merger with God. It is an Act of Grace that can only transpire after a process of purifying, healing en renewing by Gods Spirit (the kundalini). In the next chapter we will have a look at another character from the Old Testament who also embraced salvation and became a new man.

4

The prophet Elijah

"I will send my messenger, who will prepare the way before me. Then suddenly the Lord you are seeking will come to his temple; the messenger of the covenant, whom you desire, will come," says the Lord Almighty.
But who can endure the day of his coming? Who can stand when he appears? For he will be like a refiner's fire or a launderer's soap.

Malachi 3:1-2

The gospels frequently make clear connections between the great prophet of the Old Testament Elijah and both John the Baptist and Jesus. In chapter 5 we will have a closer look at a few verses in which this occurs, but first we will investigate the prophet Elijah: who was he, and can he cast more light upon the case of John and Jesus?

Elijah's existence is shrouded in mystery. Both his appearance upon the Biblical stage and his departure from it are abrupt and spectacular. His ethnonym, the Tishbite, is an enigma. He performs miracles that bring to mind the stories told about Jesus. He raises the son of a widow from the dead and causes a bowl of flour and a jar of oil never to deplete.

Who is this man who is fed by ravens and angels, and whose name makes mighty kings shudder? Upon his word the heavens shut for three and a half years and a famine breaks out in the land. Who, apart from God himself, possesses so much power and might?

In this chapter I will argue that the prophet Elijah was not a man of flesh and blood, but rather a symbol for the kundalini-energy (the Shekinah in Jewish mysticism). The Biblical stories about him are no reportages of historical events, but give us insight in the process of kundalini-awakening. Elijah's allegorical biography shines a light upon the path which God travels with us when we seek Him.

King Ahab and the idol Baal

When Elijah appears on the Biblical stage, the Israelites have succumbed to idolatry and other behavior that goes against the will of God. King Ahab, who rules at that time, is even worse than his predecessors:

Ahab son of Omri did more evil in the eyes of the Lord than any of those before him.
He not only considered it trivial to commit the sins of Jeroboam son of Nebat, but he also married Jezebel daughter of Ethbaal king of the Sidonians, and began to serve Baal and worship him.
He set up an altar for Baal in the temple of Baal that he built in Samaria.

1 Kings 17

1 And Elijah the Tishbite, who was of the inhabitants of Gilead, said unto Ahab, As the Lord God of Israel liveth, before whom I stand, there shall not be dew nor rain these years, but according to my word.

2 And the word of the Lord came unto him, saying,

3 Get thee hence, and turn thee eastward, and hide thyself by the brook Cherith, that is before Jordan.

4 And it shall be, that thou shalt drink of the brook; and I have commanded the ravens to feed thee there.

5 So he went and did according unto the word of the Lord: for he went and dwelt by the brook Cherith, that is before Jordan.

6 And the ravens brought him bread and flesh in the morning, and bread and flesh in the evening; and he drank of the brook.

7 And it came to pass after a while, that the brook dried up, because there had been no rain in the land.

8 And the word of the Lord came unto him, saying,

9 Arise, get thee to Zarephath, which belongeth to Zidon, and dwell there: behold, I have commanded a widow woman there to sustain thee.

10 So he arose and went to Zarephath. And when he came to the gate of the city, behold, the widow woman was there gathering of sticks: and he called to her, and said, Fetch me, I pray thee, a little water in a vessel, that I may drink.

11 And as she was going to fetch it, he called to her, and said, Bring me, I pray thee, a morsel of bread in thine hand.

12 And she said, As the Lord thy God liveth, I have not a cake, but an handful of meal in a barrel, and a little oil in a cruse: and, behold, I am gathering two sticks, that I may go in and dress it for me and my son, that we may eat it, and die.

13 And Elijah said unto her, Fear not; go and do as thou hast said: but make me thereof a little cake first, and bring it unto me, and after make for thee and for thy son.

14 For thus saith the Lord God of Israel, The barrel of meal shall not waste, neither shall the cruse of oil fail, until the day that the Lord sendeth rain upon the earth.

15 And she went and did according to the saying of Elijah: and she, and he, and her house, did eat many days.

16 And the barrel of meal wasted not, neither did the cruse of oil fail, according to the word of the Lord, which he spake by Elijah.

17 And it came to pass after these things, that the son of the woman, the mistress of the house, fell sick; and his sickness was so sore, that there was no breath left in him.

Ahab also made an Asherah pole and did more to arouse the anger of the Lord, the God of Israel, than did all the kings of Israel before him.
(1 Kings 16:30-33)

King Ahab represents man's ego, which descends to the animal level. The idol Baal represents the lower nature, with which the ego has connected itself. Ahab's marriage with the infamous Jezebel – whose name derives from the name Baal – symbolizes this connection.

Baal was in the ancient Middle East the supreme deity of many peoples. He was, among other things, the god of fertility, and the worship of him coincided frequently with debauchery and depravity. The battle between the supporters of Baal and those of Yahweh is a reoccurring theme in the Old Testament, and serves as a symbol for our internal battle between our lower and higher natures. The dynamic between King Ahab and Elijah reflects this.

The entree of Elijah
Out of nowhere, Elijah pops up in front of Ahab and confidently predicts a drought of years, which would not end but by his word – which he would utter in the name of Yahweh (1 Kings 17:1). What kind of man has the gall and confidence to foretell such doom in the face of a mighty king, and then stroll out of the palace unscathed?

It's an improbable situation, but with a beautiful meaning when we translate the confrontation between these two men toward an internal process. If a person (in this case Ahab) chooses for Baal (the lower nature), God withdraws. The "heavens" are shut; the rain stops. In other words: the kundalini-energy – in the Bible often presented as water – withdraws into the pelvis. And man is subsequently tormented by an inner "drought" and spiritual "famine."

The drought in Israel lasts three and a half years, which is highly significant. The Hebrew word for year, *shana*, closely resembles the word for sleep, *shena*. Eastern traditions often depict the inactive or "sleeping" kundalini as a serpent which lies coiled up in three and a half turn. Jesus mentions this number explicitly in the gospels:

18 And she said unto Elijah, What have I to do with thee, O thou man of God? art thou come unto me to call my sin to remembrance, and to slay my son?

19 And he said unto her, Give me thy son. And he took him out of her bosom, and carried him up into a loft, where he abode, and laid him upon his own bed.

20 And he cried unto the Lord, and said, O Lord my God, hast thou also brought evil upon the widow with whom I sojourn, by slaying her son?

21 And he stretched himself upon the child three times, and cried unto the Lord, and said, O Lord my God, I pray thee, let this child's soul come into him again.

22 And the Lord heard the voice of Elijah; and the soul of the child came into him again, and he revived.

23 And Elijah took the child, and brought him down out of the chamber into the house, and delivered him unto his mother: and Elijah said, See, thy son liveth.

24 And the woman said to Elijah, Now by this I know that thou art a man of God, and that the word of the Lord in thy mouth is truth.

(1 Kings 17:1-24, KJV)

*I assure you that there were many widows in Israel in Elijah's time, when **the sky was shut for three and a half years** and there was a severe famine throughout the land. Yet Elijah was not sent to any of them, but to a widow in Zarephath in the region of Sidon.*
(Luke 4:25-26)

The Hebrew word for widow also covered divorcees – divorcees were called "widows of living." in Biblical symbolic jargon, a widow is someone who does not experience a living connection with God (yet). Widowhood is a state of the soul, and since the soul is feminine, or "receiving," even a masculine person can have a "widowed soul" and be a widow. Jesus' observation that there were many widows during the (spiritual) famine is equally relevant and significant.

Elijah the indweller
In 1 Kings 17:1 Elijah is called a Tishbite, but what a Tishbite might be is utterly unclear. It looks like an ethnonym – and may refer to Elijah's hometown or even an ancestor named Tishbe – but is also virtually the same as the Hebrew word for inhabitant(s), which directly follows our ethnonym.

1 Kings 17:1 may very well mean "Elijah the inhabitant of the inhabitants of Gilead." Both the formulation and the words chosen to describe Elijah's origin are deliberately curious and reflect the mystical secret that Elijah is a personification of the "inhabitant" God, the kundalini-energy, the Shekinah.

Gilead is a rough and mountainous region east of the Jordan River. In symbolic jargon, mountains represent an expanded consciousness. The name Gilead means "Perpetual Fountain." In both eastern and western spiritual traditions the image of a fountain is often used to symbolize a change of brain fluids caused by the kundalini (think for instance of the mythical "fountain of youth"). Balsam too is used as metaphor for sublimated brain fluids. Elsewhere in the Bible the prophet Jeremiah sighs:

Is there no balm in Gilead?
Is there no physician there?
Why then is there no healing

101

for the wound of my people?
(Jeremiah 8:22)

The term "my people" refers to the people of Israel, and apparently this balsam was thought potent enough to heal a whole nation. The sources don't exactly state the ingredients of this mysterious and famous balsam from Gilead, but to the readers of this book it will be clear. It is not something that human hands can manufacture, or something that can be purchased. One receives this healing balsam internally, mercifully from God, after climbing the mountains of Gilead.

The name Elijah

The name Elijah is a combination of the word *El*, which means "God," and *Yah*, which is short for Yahweh, the personal name of God. The name Elijah, therefore, means "Yahweh is God."
The first words Elijah speaks in the Bible are: *"As the Lord God of Israel liveth, before whom I stand …"* (verse 1). A rather bold assertion: I stand before God. What mere man can and dares to say something like that? Elijah's name and his words convey that Elijah represents an aspect of God himself.

Elijah hides from King Ahab

Elijah's name, epithet, and dramatic introduction in the Biblical narrative all indicate that the prophet represents the kundalini-energy. The imagery of the subsequent verses matches this. After his visit to Ahab, God tells Elijah that he has to go into hiding, that is to say: the kundalini "retracts" into the pelvis. The name of the brook where Elijah hides is *Cherith*, which means to cut or sever, i.e. man (Ahab) is severed from God.

The story adds that when Elijah goes into hiding, he is fed by ravens (verse 4). This has made many an eyebrow rise. To the Jews, ravens were unclean animals. Why would God send unclean animals to feed Elijah? Why not, for instance, angels, as He does a bit later in the Bible (1 Kings 19:5-8)? The "unclean" birds indicate the living out of one's lower nature (Ahab's behavior).
This meaning is confirmed by the Hebrew word for raven *'oreb*. This word is highly similar to the word for mixture or impurity (*'ereb*), and the word for

nomad (*'arabi*). From the latter comes the name Arabia, which belongs to the proverbial desert peninsula, and serves in the Bible often to symbolize social or mental decentralization. It's no coincidence that both Moses and Paul spent their post-conversion years "in Arabia" (Ex 2:15, Gal 1:17) and many a Biblical hero's formative period coincides with a stint in the desert. As birds in general represent the spiritual, the ravens represent a state of spiritual bewilderment, of being without foothold, focus or objective.

In the story of Noah and the great flood (Gen 8:6-12), Noah first lets out a raven through the window after the flood has stopped. It doesn't return but keeps flying to and fro. The raven, which can't find a branch to rest on, represents the restless, impure spirit of a person in whom the kundalini process is not yet completed. Then Noah releases a dove, which initially returns carrying an olive branch in her beak, but which does not return the third time. The dove represents the purified spirit which is peaceful and stable. "Three times" represents completion. The olive branch refers to the Tree of Life from Paradise, the fruits of which yield eternal life with God. In this story, the transition from raven to dove illustrates in imagery the kundalini transformation process.

Elijah and the widow

The events of 1 Kings 17:7-24 give us a picture of the transformation process within the sincere God-seeker, personified in the widow of Zarephath. The story does not provide us with her a name, and that is usually a sign that the story is not about a specific person but rather contains a message for all of us.

The name of the widow's town, Zarephath, comes from the Hebrew *tsaraph*, and means "someone who purifies." A gold smith who smelts and refines precious metals is called a *tsorephi*. Just like in alchemy, this refining can also be translated toward an internal purification, which is required to realize the Divine gold. From what follows, the widow of Zarephath appears indeed to be an alchemist, in the spiritual sense. By her pure way of living, she has made herself worthy of Divine initiation.

Elijah is fed by ravens

In the Book of Revelation we read the following statement of Jesus: I counsel you to buy from me gold refined in the fire, so you can become rich; and white clothes to wear, so you can cover your shameful nakedness; and salve to put on your eyes, so you can see. (Rev 3:18)

In verse 9 God tells Elijah to arise. This is a command to the kundalini-energy to awaken in the widow. In verse 10, Elijah indeed rises up and goes to Zarephath (i.e. the process of purification begins).

Gathering wood by the city gate

Elijah finds the widow by the gate of the city. A door is a classic symbol for a transition to something new. The Bible often uses the image of a city gate for a Divine initiation. In the gospels, Jesus raises the deceased son of a widow back to life, just as he is carried out the city gate (Luke 7:11-17). To leave a city refers symbolically to departing from "the world"; to the letting go of a life focused on material things.

Then follow some more clear references to the kundalini process. The widow of Zarephath is gathering sticks (verse 10). The Hebrew word that is used here ('ets), means both wood and tree. The same word is used in Genesis for the Tree of Knowledge of Good and Evil, which stood in the midst of Paradise; the tree with the forbidden fruits of which Adam and Eve ate anyway. This tree represents the *ida-* and *pingala-nadi*, and hence duality[7].

The widow says in verse 12: *I am gathering **two** sticks*, that is to say: *I'm making two nadis into one ... !* She continues: *... that we may eat it, and die.* In other words: after the merging of the two *nadis*, the ego will die. This explains why Elijah has no problem with asking the widow to yield her last bit of meal and prepare him a cake (verse 13). That would have been rather dubious if we were to take this text literal. Let alone the curious fact that God sends Elijah to a widow so that she may sustain him, while she isn't even able to sustain herself.

105

Jesus brings the son of a widow back to life at a city gate

The barrel of flour and the cruse of oil that don't deplete

The exclamation of the widow in verse 12 is very interesting: *"As the Lord thy God liveth…"* She lives in the territory of the gentiles, so we may assume that she is not Jewish. Another clue is that she speaks of "your" God. How does she know that Elijah is Jewish? And more importantly: it is rather improbable that a gentile, who worships other gods, spontaneously exclaims to a stranger that his God is a *living*, and thus truly existing, God.

Also her exclamation refers to the kundalini, which is the living God within man. This kundalini, which has arisen in the widow, will feed her henceforth. That is the meaning of the meal in the barrel and the cruse of oil that will not run out (verses 14-16).

Olive oil, like balsam, is one of the Biblical metaphors for *amrita*, which is produced in the brain due to a kundalini-awakening. A jar often symbolizes man himself. "In the awakened man, the amrita will flow without ceasing," Elijah therefore actually says.

In all four gospels we read the story of Jesus' miraculous multiplication of bread. During a discourse of Jesus on a mountain the baskets of bread and fish do not go empty. That has the same significance as Elijah's flour and oil miracle, and refers to being "satisfied" by God – by means of the production of amrita and by His presence.

The necessity of self-emptying

Elijah asks the widow to use her last little bit of meal to make a cake for him, which refers to the necessity of complete, spiritual self-emptying for God to be able to complete his work in us. Sacrificing one's last possessions to God (in this case in the form of Elijah) refers to the "sacrificing" of one's ego.

The ill son of the widow

After some time, the son of the widow falls seriously ill. He too remains nameless and the story does not divulge what precisely is wrong with him. The boy represents the Divine potential in our soul; the Divine "spark," with which everybody is born. The spiritual path consists of awakening this Di-

20 So Ahab sent unto all the children of Israel, and gathered the prophets together unto mount Carmel.

21 And Elijah came unto all the people, and said, How long halt ye between two opinions? if the Lord be God, follow him: but if Baal, then follow him. And the people answered him not a word.

22 Then said Elijah unto the people, I, even I only, remain a prophet of the Lord; but Baal's prophets are four hundred and fifty men.

23 Let them therefore give us two bullocks; and let them choose one bullock for themselves, and cut it in pieces, and lay it on wood, and put no fire under: and I will dress the other bullock, and lay it on wood, and put no fire under:

24 And call ye on the name of your gods, and I will call on the name of the Lord: and the God that answereth by fire, let him be God. And all the people answered and said, It is well spoken.

25 And Elijah said unto the prophets of Baal, Choose you one bullock for yourselves, and dress it first; for ye are many; and call on the name of your gods, but put no fire under.

26 And they took the bullock which was given them, and they dressed it, and called on the name of Baal from morning even until noon, saying, O Baal, hear us. But there was no voice, nor any that answered. And they leaped upon the altar which was made.

27 And it came to pass at noon, that Elijah mocked them, and said, Cry aloud: for he is a god; either he is talking, or he is pursuing, or he is in a journey, or peradventure he sleepeth, and must be awaked.

28 And they cried aloud, and cut themselves after their manner with knives and lancets, till the blood gushed out upon them.

29 And it came to pass, when midday was past, and they prophesied until the time of the offering of the evening sacrifice, that there was neither voice, nor any to answer, nor any that regarded.

30 And Elijah said unto all the people, Come near unto me. And all the people came near unto him. And he repaired the altar of the Lord that was broken down.

31 And Elijah took twelve stones, according to the number of the tribes of the sons of Jacob, unto whom the word of the Lord came, saying, Israel shall be thy name:

32 And with the stones he built an altar in the name of the Lord: and he made a trench about the altar, as great as would contain two measures of seed.

33 And he put the wood in order, and cut the bullock in pieces, and laid him on the wood, and said, Fill four barrels with water, and pour it on the burnt sacrifice, and on the wood.

34 And he said, Do it the second time. And they did it the second time. And he said, Do it the third time. And they did it the third time.

vine spark and letting it grow into what is called a "Christ consciousness." In people who are focused on material things and are not interested in spiritual growth, this Divine principle suffers a sleeping or "pining" existence.

In the gospel of Mark, Jesus compliments a poor widow who submits her last few coins to the offering box of the temple (Mark 12:42-44). That raises questions since he, just a few verses earlier, accuses the Pharisees of enriching themselves at the cost of widows (Mark 12:38-40). Here too we are looking at spiritual self-emptying. The poverty of the widow refers to her spirit: the releasing of one's ego to find God. Jesus mentions being poor in spirit as initial virtue in his famous Sermon on the Mount: Blessed are the poor in spirit for theirs is the Kingdom of heaven (Matt. 5:3).

Elijah, who revives the son of the widow, shows us how the purifying kundalini-energy creates the right circumstances for the birth of the Divine child, or "Christ child" in our soul. This takes place only after the kundalini has arrived at the sixth and seventh chakra, which is hinted at in the statement that he *carried him up into a loft, where he abode* ...(verse 19).

And he stretched himself upon the child three times... (verse 21), which refers to a completed kundalini process. Three times refers to "completely." The image of Elijah stretching himself out on the boy demonstrates how the kundalini-energy performs her healing and purifying work in the *entire* person. In a later chapter of the Bible, Elijah's successor Elisha will do something highly similar:

When Elisha reached the house, there was the boy lying dead on his couch.
He went in, shut the door on the two of them and prayed to the Lord.
Then he got on the bed and lay on the boy, mouth to mouth, eyes to eyes, hands to hands. As he stretched himself out on him, the boy's body grew warm.
Elisha turned away and walked back and forth in the room and then got on the bed and stretched out on him once more. The boy sneezed seven times and opened his eyes.
(2 Kings 4:32-35)

35 And the water ran round about the altar; and he filled the trench also with water.

36 And it came to pass at the time of the offering of the evening sacrifice, that Elijah the prophet came near, and said, Lord God of Abraham, Isaac, and of Israel, let it be known this day that thou art God in Israel, and that I am thy servant, and that I have done all these things at thy word.

37 Hear me, O Lord, hear me, that this people may know that thou art the Lord God, and that thou hast turned their heart back again.

38 Then the fire of the Lord fell, and consumed the burnt sacrifice, and the wood, and the stones, and the dust, and licked up the water that was in the trench.

39 And when all the people saw it, they fell on their faces: and they said, The Lord, he is the God; the Lord, he is the God.

40 And Elijah said unto them, Take the prophets of Baal; let not one of them escape. And they took them: and Elijah brought them down to the brook Kishon, and slew them there.

41 And Elijah said unto Ahab, Get thee up, eat and drink; for there is a sound of abundance of rain.

42 So Ahab went up to eat and to drink. And Elijah went up to the top of Carmel; and he cast himself down upon the earth, and put his face between his knees,

43 And said to his servant, Go up now, look toward the sea. And he went up, and looked, and said, There is nothing. And he said, Go again seven times.

44 And it came to pass at the seventh time, that he said, Behold, there ariseth a little cloud out of the sea, like a man's hand. And he said, Go up, say unto Ahab, Prepare thy chariot, and get thee down that the rain stop thee not.

45 And it came to pass in the mean while, that the heaven was black with clouds and wind, and there was a great rain. And Ahab rode, and went to Jezreel.

46 And the hand of the Lord was on Elijah; and he girded up his loins, and ran before Ahab to the entrance of Jezreel.

(1 Kings 18:20-46, KJV)

Here the kundalini-symbolism is even clearer: Elisha who walks back and forth in the room illustrates the *modus operandi* of the Divine energy in a person's entire body. The seven times sneezing refers to the activation of the seven chakras, after which the Divine (in the soul) can come to life. We'll talk more about this successor of Elijah later!

> **In the gospels** Jesus brings two deceased children back to life. The twelve year old daughter of the chief of the synagogue, Jairus[8] (Mark 5:21-43, Matt. 9:18-26, and Luke 8:40-56), and the previously mentioned resurrection of the son of the widow at the city gate (Luke 7:11-17). Both stories are about the bringing to life of the Divine child in the soul of man.

Elijah and the prophets of Baal

After the story of the widow of Zarephath and her son follows a colorful account of the famous clash between Elijah and the prophets of Baal. It is three years later and God says to Elijah: *Go and show yourself to Ahab, and I will send rain on the earth* (1 Kings 18:1). Elijah emerges from hiding, and having arrived at Ahab's he orders him to assemble all the people of Israel and the prophets of Baal on the holy mountain Carmel.

Elijah challenges the prophets of Baal to a showdown to determine who the true God is: Yahweh or Baal. Two altars are prepared; both with a young bull as sacrifice. The one who answers the call and kindles the wood will be the true God (verse 24).

> **In the Book of Exodus** Moses becomes furious when he discovers that the Israelites are worshipping a golden bull calf, despite the first of the Ten Commandments: You shall have no other gods before Me (Ex. 20:3 and Ex. 32:3-4). The worship of the golden calf symbolizes man's enslavement to the desires of his body and his forgetting of his higher nature. The Israelites had manufactured this golden calf from smelted gold earrings they had worn: jewelry is intended to adorn the body and is a sign of vanity.

111

Moses becomes furious when he discovers that the Israelites are worshipping a golden bull calf.

A bull symbolizes our animal nature. Not only in the Bible but also in Hinduism for instance, where the god Shiva is often depicted along his white bull Nandi. This bull symbolizes the purified animal forces of Shiva.

When the prodigal son of Jesus' familiar parable returns to his father (God), the latter orders the fattened calf slaughtered (Luke 15:11-32). Here too the calf represents the animal nature which the boy (the spiritual seeker) has conquered with the help of God.

Animal sacrifices were widely customary in many traditions and represent the "sacrificing" of one's animal nature. As we saw earlier, Baal, the god of fertility, represents in the Bible man's lower nature. The showdown between the prophet of Yahweh and those of Baal – like most wars and battles in the Bible – is about man's inner struggle between his higher and lower natures.

The altar as symbol of the heart

The altar with the bull that the prophets of Baal erect doesn't catch fire, but the altar of Elijah does. This shows us that the fire of the kundalini (Elijah) purifies our animal nature. The twelve stones from which Elijah builds his altar (verse 31), represent the twelve "petals" or *nadis* of the heart chakra, which tells us that the altar symbolizes man's heart.

Heart chakra

113

Elijah calls upon God and his sacrifice ignites

In the Book of Joshua we read: *Joshua set up the twelve stones that had been in the middle of the Jordan at the spot where the priests who carried the Ark of the Covenant had stood. And they are there to this day* (Joshua 4:9).
The twelve stones of Joshua refer to the heart chakra, which is located in the middle of the *sushumna-nadi* (the Jordan River) in the spinal column[9].

The trench which Elijah digs around the altar refers to the circulatory system (verse 32). The four barrels (verse 33) represent the four chambers of the physical heart: the upper left and right atria and lower left and right ventricles. The water from the four barrels that flows over the altar and fills the surrounding trench (verse 35), symbolizes the blood that the heart pumps through the body.

The trench was large enough to contain two measures of seed (verse 32). This rather curious way to declare the size of a ditch is obviously a metaphor, and the word "seed" is representative of the "fruits" of a person; his behavior and deeds. These stem from his dualistic higher and lower natures (the two measures). This same duality is expressed in Elijah's question to the Israelites: *How long halt ye between two opinions?* (verse 21).

At the beckoning of Elijah, fire from God came down and consumes everything: *the burnt sacrifice, and the wood, and the stones, and the dust, and licked up the water that was in the trench* (verse 38). The kundalini-fire purifies the entire man on all levels: physical, emotional, mental and energetic.

To confirm that this whole affair concerns the purging of the animalistic, Elijah kills all the prophets of Baal, in disregard of the sixth Commandment that clearly states: *You will not murder.* Elijah's personal massacre of four hundred and fifty men is again a metaphor.

The name Kishon, which belongs to the brook where the slaying of the Baal priests takes place (verse 40), comes from the Hebrew verb *yaqosh*, which means "to lay bait" or "a laying of a trap to catch animals." Elijah killed all

Elijah Flees to Horeb

4 ... while he himself went a day's journey into the wilderness. He came to a broom bush, sat down under it and prayed that he might die. "I have had enough, Lord," he said. "Take my life; I am no better than my ancestors."

5 Then he lay down under the bush and fell asleep.

All at once an angel touched him and said, "Get up and eat."

6 He looked around, and there by his head was some bread baked over hot coals, and a jar of water. He ate and drank and then lay down again.

7 The angel of the Lord came back a second time and touched him and said, "Get up and eat, for the journey is too much for you."

8 So he got up and ate and drank. Strengthened by that food, he traveled forty days and forty nights until he reached Horeb, the mountain of God.

9 There he went into a cave and spent the night.

The Lord Appears to Elijah

And the word of the Lord came to him: "What are you doing here, Elijah?"

10 He replied, "I have been very zealous for the Lord God Almighty. The Israelites have rejected your covenant, torn down your altars, and put your prophets to death with the sword. I am the only one left, and now they are trying to kill me too."

11 The Lord said, "Go out and stand on the mountain in the presence of the Lord, for the Lord is about to pass by."

Then a great and powerful wind tore the mountains apart and shattered the rocks before the Lord, but the Lord was not in the wind. After the wind there was an earthquake, but the Lord was not in the earthquake.

12 After the earthquake came a fire, but the Lord was not in the fire. And after the fire came a gentle whisper.

13 When Elijah heard it, he pulled his cloak over his face and went out and stood at the mouth of the cave.

Then a voice said to him, "What are you doing here, Elijah?"

(1 Kings 19:4-13)

prophets with the sword (1 Kings 19:1); the sword is one of the symbols for the spinal column with inside the active kundalini-energy.

> **In the Book of 1 Samuel of the Old Testament,** David, the future king of Israel and then still a shepherd, wages a battle with his ego, and, connected to it, his lower nature, symbolized in Goliath. After he has felled the ferocious giant with a stone to the forehead (the sixth chakra), he lobs off his head with a sword (1 Samuel 17:48-51). A head that gets chopped off is a universal metaphor for the death of the ego as result of a kundalini-awakening.

The hand of God

The victory over the prophets of Baal rang in the end of the drought and famine in the land, because afterward Elijah says to Ahab: "*Get thee up, eat and drink; for there is a sound of abundance of rain.*" (verse 41). The magnificent imagery of verses 41 through 46 makes it clear that this predicted rain is a kundalini-awakening, through which man's spiritual thirst is quenched.

Elijah casts himself down upon the earth and puts his face between his knees (verse 42), which illustrates the kundalini-energy coiled up in the pelvis. Seven times Elijah instructs his servant to climb up to the top of the mountain (verse 43), which corresponds with the kundalini-energy that rises through the seven chakras to the crown. After the seventh time, a small cloud "*like a man's hand*" rises from the sea, upon which it starts to rain (verse 44-45). This hand is the hand of God and refers to the kundalini-energy. Two verses later we read: *And the hand of the Lord was on Elijah* (verse 46). With this the author is saying: the hand of the Lord *is* Elijah, *is* the kundalini-energy.

The loins girded

Elijah subsequently girds his loins (verse 46). This symbolizes mastery over the animal nature. In the next chapter of the Bible we find a description of the appearance of Elijah which confirms this. King Ahab asks his emissaries:

7   *The king asked them, "What kind of man was it who came to meet you and told you this?"*

8   *They replied, "He had a garment of hair and had a leather belt around his waist."*
    (2 Kings 1:7-8, NIV)

John the Baptist too wore garments made of animal hair and wore a leather belt around his waist (Matt. 3:4). In symbolic jargon, someone's clothing describes his personality or spiritual level. Wearing an animal hide symbolizes living out the animal instincts. Combined with a belt about the loins it means the wearer has control over his animal nature.

In the gospel of Luke Jesus says to his disciples, *"Let your loins be girded about, and your lights burning; And ye yourselves like unto men that wait for their lord, when he will return from the wedding; that when he cometh and knocketh, they may open unto him immediately."* (Luke 12:35-36, King James Version).
The lamps are the chakras. Jesus advises his disciples (and us) to not waste our sexual energy on animal instincts, but to keep it as nutrition for the chakras, so that they (and we) will be ready for God, when He comes.

Elijah wishes to die

When Jezebel, the wife of Ahab, hears that Elijah has killed all the prophets of Baal, she wants to have him assassinated. Elijah flees into the desert, sits down under a broom bush, and prays to God that he may die (1 Kings 19:1-4). We have arrived at the next phase of the kundalini-process. Now that the animal nature has been conquered, it's the ego's turn to "die."

This specific bush (*Retama raetam*) is a desert shrub which is a known source of fuel. When charred, the wood of this shrub turns to a high caloric coal. It's therefore a perfectly suited metaphor for the "kundalini-tree."

While under the broom bush, Elijah is fed by an angel (instead of ravens, as earlier). The angel wakes him and commands him to stand up. Elijah discovers by his head some baked bread and a jar of water (verse 6). We again recognize in these images the kundalini-process in a nutshell.

Elijah who is asleep under the shrub symbolizes the kundalini sleeping in the pelvis. God (in the form of an angel) wakes the kundalini and makes it rise, upon which in the brain ("by the head") substances are released which nourish the awakened person physically and spiritually. The brain fluid changes into *amrita*, the elixir of immortality of eastern traditions, or *ambrosia*, the food of the gods of Greece. The hot coals on which the divine bread is baked symbolize the kundalini fire.

Then Elijah traverses the desert for forty days to ultimately arrive at Mount Horeb, the mountain of God (verse 8). In physical reality, this journey could have been accomplished in three days, and Elijah's forty day journey tells of a spiritual trek. As we saw in the previous chapter, the number forty symbolizes a period of spiritual transition. Moses receives the stone tablets with the Ten Commandments after fasting forty days on Mount Horeb. The people of Moses roam the desert for forty years, looking for the Promised Land. Jesus stays in the desert forty days after his baptism in the Jordan River. Forty is the product of four times ten and represents the perfecting (ten) of the four aspects of man: body, mind, heart, and soul. The number forty combined with a unit of time (days, months or years) symbolizes a transformation process.

The encounter with God on Horeb

After forty days in the desert, Elijah encounters God in a cave on Mount Horeb (verse 9); the same mountain on which Moses had an encounter with God. The summit of a mountain represents the head. The Hebrew source text speaks of *the* cave and not *a* cave. The cave in which Elijah lodges is what the eastern traditions call *the cave of Brahman*; the thalamus region of the brain (thalamus and hypothalamus). The place in the brain which allows us to experience God and communicate with Him.

The Greek word *thalamos* means "inner chamber"; in antiquity it was assumed that there the spirit of a person lodged. This area of the brain is sometimes referred to as the "bridal chamber" because there the union (the sacred marriage) between God and man takes place. It is also the place where the *ida-* and *pingala-nadi* (bride and groom) merge.

Elijah on Mount Horeb

Elijah's encounter with God is equally poetic as it is dramatic. On the top of the mountain, Elijah first experiences a strong wind pass by, which splits mountains and breaks rocks, then an earthquake and finally a fire (verse 11-12). These impressive images describe the internal effects of the kundalini-energy; the person (the mountain) is "broken open," purified and transformed.

After this violence of nature comes silence. This is the inner tranquility which a person experiences after the completion of the kundalini-process; when the swamp of the subconscious is drained and no thoughts remain to ripple one's perfectly clear consciousness. In the whisper of this gentle silence Elijah hears the voice of God (verse 12-13).

In the Book of Revelation we read about a silence of half an hour, which commences when the seventh and final seal (chakra) of the scroll (spine) breaks: *When he opened the seventh seal, there was silence in heaven for about half an hour* (Revelation 8:1).

Elijah's ego has "disappeared"; it has become invisible, which is symbolized by the cloak which Elijah wraps around his face (verse 13). The purified ego is totally transparent, and therefore seems absent.

In the gospel of John, Jesus uses the image of the wind to describe the transparency of the ego after the rebirth: *The wind blows wherever it pleases. You hear its sound, but you cannot tell where it comes from or where it is going. So it is with everyone born of the Spirit* (John 3:7-8).

Elisha, the successor of Elijah

Immediately after the "disappearance" of Elijah's ego on Mount Horeb, he is succeeded by Elisha. Like the names Joshua and Jesus, the name Elisha incorporates the verb *yasha*, to save, and means God is Salvation, which is basically similar to the meaning of Joshua and Jesus: YHWH is salvation.

True to the pattern in which Joshua succeeds Moses and Jesus succeeds

121

Elijah Taken Up to Heaven

7 Fifty men from the company of the prophets went and stood at a distance, facing the place where Elijah and Elisha had stopped at the Jordan.

8 Elijah took his cloak, rolled it up and struck the water with it. The water divided to the right and to the left, and the two of them crossed over on dry ground.

9 When they had crossed, Elijah said to Elisha, "Tell me, what can I do for you before I am taken from you?"

"Let me inherit a double portion of your spirit," Elisha replied.

10 "You have asked a difficult thing," Elijah said, "yet if you see me when I am taken from you, it will be yours—otherwise, it will not."

11 As they were walking along and talking together, suddenly a chariot of fire and horses of fire appeared and separated the two of them, and Elijah went up to heaven in a whirlwind.

12 Elisha saw this and cried out, "My father! My father! The chariots and horsemen of Israel!" And Elisha saw him no more. Then he took hold of his garment and tore it in two.

13 Elisha then picked up Elijah's cloak that had fallen from him and went back and stood on the bank of the Jordan.

14 He took the cloak that had fallen from Elijah and struck the water with it. "Where now is the Lord, the God of Elijah?" he asked. When he struck the water, it divided to the right and to the left, and he crossed over.

15 The company of the prophets from Jericho, who were watching, said, "The spirit of Elijah is resting on Elisha." And they went to meet him and bowed to the ground before him.

(2 Kings 2:7-15)

John, Elisha not simply follows Elijah but is the reborn version of Elijah. That is why, at their initial encounter Elijah gives his cloak to Elisha: *Elijah went up to him and threw his cloak around him* (1 Kings 19:19). The source text of this passage literally says: *Elijah crossed over to him ...* As we saw earlier, a crossing over is a metaphor for a transformation.

Elijah ascends into heaven

Immediately after his encounter with Elisha, Elijah disappears in a spectacular way. The story is full of transformation symbolism; the reader will doubtlessly recognize many. The Jordan, where the ascension of Elijah takes place (page 122, verse 7), represents the *sushumna-nadi*, the meridian through which the kundalini-energy flows toward the crown (heaven).

Several details of the story point toward the process of integration of the higher and lower natures – the purified animal forces are the engine for the realization of the higher nature. This process is an important aspect of a spiritual rebirth. Elisha's mysterious request as recorded in verse 9 ("*Let me inherit a double portion of your spirit*") refers to this. The duality which Elijah, the old man, still experiences will shortly become one in Elisha.

Also the garments he tears in two (verse 12) symbolizes the dual nature. After he does this, he picks up the (intact) cloak which has fallen off Elijah; a symbol of oneness and integration. Elisha thus goes from duality to unity. The exchange of the cloak between owners additionally represents the transformation of Elijah into Elisha. Then Elisha does the same thing with this cloak as Elijah did just previously: *... he struck the water, it divided to the right and to the left ...* (verses 8 and 14).

The dividing of the waters of the Jordan also refers to the dual nature of man. The first time this happens in the story, both Elijah and Elisha cross over. The second time only Elisha crosses: the integration has taken place. Crossing the Jordan without getting wet metaphorizes also another aspect of the kundalini-process, namely the mastery over the emotions. Water is the archetypal image of man's emotional life and subconscious. Walking to the opposite side of a river and staying dry means that one is no longer affected by one's inner stirrings.

Elijah ascends into heaven in a whirlwind

In the gospels we find the spectacular and overly familiar account of Jesus who walks on water toward his disciples. This too is symbolism, just like the crossing of the Jordan, and demonstrates that Jesus had mastered his emotions.

When in the Book of Exodus Moses raises his staff (the kundalini), the Red Sea splits into two halves, which allows the Israelites to cross over to the far side (Ex. 14:21-22).

The chariot of fire with horses of fire, which separates Elijah from Elisha (verse 11), symbolizes the kundalini-energy and the sublimated animal forces, which bring about the rebirth. Also the whirlwind which carries Elijah into the heavens is a depiction of the whirling kundalini-energy which flows upward toward the opened crown chakra.

The words of the cadet prophets of verse 15 summarize what happened: *The spirit of Elijah is resting upon Elisha.* Elijah continues his life as Elisha.

Finally, also the presence of *fifty* men from the company of prophets (verse 7) shows that this story is about the dual nature of man and a kundalini-awakening (see for a discussion of the meaning of the number fifty chapter 3).

Elisha in the footsteps of Elijah
Both in words and in actions Elisha is similar to his predecessor Elijah. Both use the introduction: *As the Lord lives, before whom I stand ...* (Elijah in 1 Kings 17:1 and Elisha in 2 Kings 3:14 and 5:16).

Elisha likewise causes a poor widow's jar of olive oil to not run out (2 Kings 4:2-5), and raises a woman's dead son back to life (2 Kings 4:32-35). Just like Elijah, Elisha collides with the ruling king of Israel.

The return of Elijah
The Book of Malachi, the final book of the Old Testament, ends with the prediction that Elijah will come again, preceding the coming of the Messiah.

See, I will send
the prophet Elijah
to you before that great and dreadful
day of the Lord comes.
(Malachi 4:5)

Jews who don't recognize Jesus as the Messiah, still eagerly look forward to the coming of the prophet. At every *brit milah* (ritual circumcision) a chair is kept open for him, and at every Passover Seder a cup is filled with wine for him.

Esoterically (internally) speaking it's correct that the Messiah is preceded by Elijah, when we regard Elijah as the personification of the kundalini, and a Messiah – an anointed one – as someone who completed the kundalini-process. The Jews, however, expect actual persons.

And so, through the ages, quite a bit of expectant waiting has been done by entire populations. The Mayas awaited the god Quetzalcoatl. The Hindus expect the avatar Kalki. And for nearly two millennia the Christians have waited for the return of Jesus.

In all these cases, the holy scriptures that predict these returns speak about an *inner* event. All of us – irrespective of creed, race or culture – are called to make a step of growth in human evolution, to attain God-consciousness and immortality.

With my books I hope to make people aware of this, so that they no longer gaze into the heavens and search for special signs in the outside world, but turn to their inside, to thus discover that all that time their Redeemer was waiting too, for them ... at the door of their heart.

5

Elijah in the gospels

To be sure, Elijah comes and will restore all things.

Matt. 17:11

The story of Elijah who becomes Elisha is an allegorical description of the factual transformation of John the Baptist into Jesus Christ. The authors of the gospels have subtly interwoven Elijah in Jesus' life story to communicate this. Let's have a look at the specific verses in which Elijah is mentioned.

Is John Elijah?

The evangelists Mark and Matthew depict John as wearing the same clothing as Elijah. Clothing in Jewish society was a complicated affair of symbols and codes, and many social functions came with specific garb. By giving John the same "uniform" as Elijah (see Zechariah 13:4), the authors deliberate equate the two. The obvious conclusion: this is Elijah for whom we have waited so long, and now the Messiah will also appear shortly!

> *Elijah ... had a garment of hair and had a leather belt around his waist.*
> (2 Kings 1:8)

> *John wore clothing made of camel's hair, with a leather belt around his waist ...*
> (Mark 1:6 and Matt. 3:4)

Jesus and John the Baptist themselves give cryptic and contradictory answers to the crucial question of whether John is Elijah. Jesus' answer is affirmative:

> *For all the Prophets and the Law prophesied until John. And if you are willing to accept it, he is the Elijah who was to come. Whoever has ears, let them hear.*
> (Matthew 11:13-15)

But John denies it:

> *They asked him, "Then who are you? Are you Elijah?" He said, "I am not." "Are you the Prophet?" He answered, "No."*
> (John 1:21)

John was only Elijah from the perspective of Jesus. From John's own perspective he was a mere voice crying out in the desert, unable to imagine either the essence of the Christ or to comprehend his own role in Christ's

The transfiguration on the mountain

coming. Jesus and John relate like butterfly and caterpillar; although they contain each other, the caterpillar understands neither and the butterfly understands both.

The evangelist Luke drops the name of Elijah in the birth announcement of John by the angel Gabriel, deliberately using the words *spirit and power* to hint at the kundalini-process that Elijah represents:

> And **he will go on before the Lord, in the spirit and power of Elijah,** *to turn the hearts of the parents to their children and the disobedient to the wisdom of the righteous—to make ready a people prepared for the Lord."*
> (Luke 1:17)

Luke also connects John to Elijah's successor Elisha. He is the only evangelist that mentions the name of the mother of John: Elizabeth (in Greek: *Elisabet*). This combination of *Elisa* and *bet*, sounded to the Jews in that time as 'house of Elisha'!

The transfiguration on the mountain

How should we interpret Elijah's appearance during the famous and mysterious transfiguration of Jesus on the mountain? Jesus takes three disciples with him onto a high mountain, where they see him transform. This metamorphosis into a radiant, white appearance seems to be a foretaste of his resurrection body, with which he resurrects after his death on the cross, and is subsequently observed with for forty days after. It's a light-body which is interwoven with his physical body, and in which the great mystery of eternal life is contained.

> 27 *"Truly I tell you, some who are standing here will not taste death before they see the kingdom of God."*
> 28 *About eight days after Jesus said this, he took Peter, John and James with him and went up onto a mountain to pray.*
> 29 *As he was praying, the appearance of his face changed, and his clothes became as bright as a flash of lightning.*
> 30 *Two men, Moses and Elijah, appeared in glorious splendor, talking with Jesus.*

> [31] *They spoke about his departure, which he was about to bring to fulfillment at Jerusalem.*
> (Luke 9:27-31)

The disciples see two men standing by Jesus during his transformation: the prophets Moses and Elijah[10]. The subject of the conversation between the three men gives us an important clue to the meaning of their presence. Luke says that Moses and Elijah *spoke* (with Jesus) *about his departure* (verse 31).

With the departure of Jesus is meant his death on the cross, which in the gospels symbolizes the dying of the ego. The subsequent resurrection from the grave represents the inner "resurrection," or the awakening of the spiritual aspirant. As we saw in the previous chapters, this transformation process is depicted in the Old Testament in the stories of Moses and Elijah. Both did not die a natural death; their bodies were taken away by God, which symbolizes the death of the old man. Moses is "buried by God" on an unknown location (Deut 34:6) and is succeeded by Joshua. Elijah is, after his "ascension" into heaven, succeeded by Elisha. The presence of Moses and Elijah during the transfiguration tells us that we should see the departure of Jesus in the same light as the departure of the two great prophets: as the inner death of the old man.

Elijah restores all things
In the gospel of Mark, the report on the transfiguration is followed by an interesting dialogue between Jesus and his three stupefied disciples.

> [9] *As they were coming down the mountain, Jesus gave them orders not to tell anyone what they had seen until the Son of Man had risen from the dead.*
> [10] *They kept the matter to themselves, discussing what "rising from the dead" meant.*
> [11] *And they asked him, "Why do the teachers of the law say that Elijah must come first?"*
> [12] *Jesus replied, "To be sure, Elijah does come first, and restores all things. Why then is it written that the Son of Man must suffer much and be rejected?*

13 *But I tell you, Elijah has come, and they have done to him everything they wished, just as it is written about him."*
(Mark 9:9-13)

Elijah not only personifies the old man in the Old Testament, he also personifies the kundalini; the Divine energy which purifies and heals the old man. Mark 9:10-12 paraphrased says: before the resurrection from the dead can take place, Elijah (the kundalini) must come first and "restore" the person.

This restoration involves a healing process which leads to wholeness, or "perfection" in the words of Jesus: *"Be perfect, therefore, as your heavenly Father is* perfect" (Matt. 5:48).

The crucifixion

The gospel writers don't only connect Elijah with the glorious moment of transfiguration on the mountain. His name is also mentioned during Jesus' deepest suffering on the cross.

45 *From noon until three in the afternoon darkness came over all the land.*
46 *About three in the afternoon Jesus cried out in a loud voice, "Eli, Eli, lema sabachthani?" (which means "My God, my God, why have you forsaken me?").*
47 *When some of those standing there heard this, they said, "He's calling Elijah."*
48 *Immediately one of them ran and got a sponge. He filled it with wine vinegar, put it on a staff, and offered it to Jesus to drink.*
49 *The rest said, "Now leave him alone. Let's see if Elijah comes to save him."*
50 *And when Jesus had cried out again in a loud voice, he gave up his spirit.*
51 *At that moment the curtain of the temple was torn in two from top to bottom. The earth shook, the rocks split*
52 *and the tombs broke open. The bodies of many holy people who had died were raised to life.*
53 *They came out of the tombs after Jesus' resurrection and went into the holy city and appeared to many people.*
54 *When the centurion and those with him who were guarding Jesus saw the*

earthquake and all that had happened, they were terrified, and exclaimed,
"Surely he was the Son of God!"
(Matt. 27:45-54)

It appears that the bystanders don't understand Jesus properly when he calls out: *Eli, Eli, lema sabachthani?* Matthew has them think that he calls out to Elijah (verse 47). This is a clever literary construction to interweave the crucifixion with kundalini-symbolism.

I do not doubt that Jesus indeed died on the cross, but ultimately the historical crucifixion served as the seed of the much larger narrative. Most of the details were added by the authors to clarify the universal way to the Kingdom of God. This also explains why there are so many differences between the four gospels.

To paraphrase Matthew:

Verse 45: The darkness that comes over the earth is the darkness in which the spiritual aspirant exists when he experiences no living connection with God (yet).

Verse 46: Jesus' desperate cry confirms the condition of being abandoned by God.

Verse 47: Elijah represents the kundalini-energy, which is being evoked.

Verse 48: The sponge with wine vinegar, which is put on a staff and brought to Jesus' mouth, is a metaphor for the kundalini-energy which ascends to the head.

Verse 49: The activated kundalini-energy *"comes to save"* the spiritual aspirant from ego and darkness.

Verse 50: The old man dies.

Verse 51: The crown chakra opens, Divine light flows in, and man is united with his Creator.

The images of an earthquake and rocks that split (verse 51), describe the effect of the kundalini-energy: the inner world of the spiritual aspirant shakes on its foundations. The person is "broken open," purified and transformed. These images are highly similar to the Divine experience of Elijah on Mount

Horeb, which also describes a kundalini-awakening – as we saw in the previous chapter.

> *The Lord said, "Go out and stand on the mountain in the presence of the Lord, for the Lord is about to pass by."*
> *Then a great and powerful wind tore the mountains apart and shattered the rocks before the Lord, but the Lord was not in the wind. After the wind there was an earthquake, but the Lord was not in the earthquake.*
> (1 Kings 19:11)

This similarity is no coincidence. Matthew deliberately interweaves these two events to convey the meaning of the crucifixion.

The Miraculous Catch of Fish

Most stories from the gospels depend heavily on material from the Old Testament. One particular example is the story of the miraculous catch of fish, which incorporates symbols and structures from the stories about Jonah and Elijah, and which also is a depiction of an internal process. In John's version of this story, the apostle Peter takes the central role and the events play after Jesus' resurrection.

The risen Jesus instructs the disciples about how to fish, and they proceed to catch precisely one hundred and fifty three fish. This story touches on all the themes we've discussed so far. Let's have a look at the details.

Meeting the risen Jesus

The author tells us from first-hand about the extraordinary encounter. As is common in the Bible, the classical metaphor of a journey to the "other side" is deployed to symbolize the way to God.

The seven disciples have arrived at the shore after a journey over water. The ship was about two hundred cubits away from shore, says verse 8. This distance metaphorizes their remaining in duality (two). It is morning (verse 4), the moment of sunrise, which is symbol for spiritual awakening. The disciples see Jesus stand on the shore without recognizing him. Here

The appearance by the Sea of Galilee

1 After these things Jesus showed Himself again to the disciples at the Sea of Tiberias, and in this way showed He Himself:

2 There were together Simon Peter, and Thomas called Didymus, and Nathanael of Cana in Galilee, and the sons of Zebedee, and two other of His disciples.

3 Simon Peter said unto them, "I am going fishing." They said unto him, "We also go with thee." They went forth and entered into a boat immediately; and that night they caught nothing.

4 But when the morning had now come, Jesus stood on the shore, but the disciples knew not that it was Jesus.

5 Then Jesus said unto them, "Children, have ye any meat?" And they answered Him, "No."

6 And He said unto them, "Cast the net on the right side of the boat, and ye shall find." They cast therefore, and now they were not able to draw it in for the multitude of fishes.

7 Therefore that disciple whom Jesus loved said unto Peter, "It is the Lord!" Now when Simon Peter heard that it was the Lord, he girded his fisher's coat unto him (for he was naked) and cast himself into the sea.

8 And the other disciples came in a little boat (for they were not far from land, but, as it were, two hundred cubits), dragging the net with fishes.

9 As soon then as they had come to land, they saw a fire of coals there, and fish laid thereon and bread.

10 Jesus said unto them, "Bring of the fish which ye have now caught."

11 Simon Peter went up and drew the net to land, full of great fishes, a hundred and fifty three; and though there were so many, yet the net was not broken.

12 Jesus said unto them, "Come and dine." And none of the disciples dared ask Him, "Who art Thou?" knowing that it was the Lord.

13 Jesus then came and took bread and gave it to them, and fish likewise.

14 This is now the third time that Jesus showed Himself to His disciples after He was risen from the dead.

15 So when they had dined, Jesus said to Simon Peter, "Simon, son of Jonah, lovest thou Me more than these?" He said unto Him, "Yea, Lord; Thou knowest that I love Thee." He said unto him, "Feed My lambs."

(John 21:1-15, KJ21)

this could perhaps be due to the lack of daylight, but it will happen more often that his own disciples don't recognize Jesus when he appears to them after his death (see John 20:14 and Luke 24:16). The obvious question this provokes is: what particular appearance did he have when he showed himself to them?

The reason why his disciples don't recognize him right away is that their meeting with Christ is an inner experience, and the event describes a kundalini-awakening. Simon Peter who leaps out the boat and into the sea (verse 7) derives from the story of Jonah, who is tossed off his ship in the middle of the sea. To make this even more obvious, Jesus calls him *Simon of Jonah* (21:15-17). Earlier, Jesus had called him "son of Jonah" (John 1:42), but now Jesus drops the son-part, thereby connecting Peter's plunge into the sea to the initiation story of Jonah. Just like the subtle note that the net, after it was cast out, was full of *great fish* (verse 11).

A naked Peter
Peter's sudden dive into the sea comes with another curious fact, namely that he first gets dressed (verse 7). Doesn't common sense dictate that he had better undressed before his jump?

The Greek word for the particular garment with which Peter dresses himself is an *ependutes*, which denotes a robe or outer garment. We find the related verb *ependuo* in Paul's second letter to the Corinthians:

> *Meanwhile we groan, longing to be clothed* [ependuo] *instead with our heavenly dwelling, because when we are clothed* [enduo], *we will not be found naked. For while we are in this tent, we groan and are burdened, because we do not wish to be unclothed* [ekduo] *but to be clothed* [ependuo] *instead with our heavenly dwelling, so that what is mortal may be swallowed up by life.*
> (2 Cor 5:2-4)

Peter's garment is the immortal light-body, or resurrection-body, which is built up during the kundalini-process. The reason why Peter dresses himself, the author submits, is that he was naked (*gumnos*). We are all naked until we are clothed with the resurrection-body:

You say, 'I am rich; I have acquired wealth and do not need a thing.' But you do not realize that you are wretched, pitiful, poor, blind and naked.
(Rev 3:17)

Several passages and parables in the gospels refer to the new clothes or wedding clothes of the awakened man. For instance: when the prodigal son from the Lucan parable returns home to his father (i.e. God) after a long journey, the latter has him dressed in "the best robe" (Luke 15:22).

Paul says it in unmitigated terms in his first letter to the Corinthians:

Listen, I tell you a mystery: We will not all sleep, but we will all be changed— in a flash, in the twinkling of an eye, at the last trumpet. For the trumpet will sound, the dead will be raised imperishable, and we will be changed. For the perishable must clothe [enduo] itself with the imperishable, and the mortal with immortality.
When the perishable has been clothed [enduo] with the imperishable, and the mortal with immortality, then the saying that is written will come true: "Death has been swallowed up in victory".
(1 Corinthians 15:51-54)

Great Fish
The disciples have caught precisely one hundred and fifty three fish according to verse 11, and this rather unpractical precision obviously hints at meaning. The exact nature of this meaning is topic of debate, but most probably, the number 153 refers to the *vesica piscis* – the ancient symbol we discussed in chapter three, of which two partially overlapping circles symbolize the merger of opposites.

The famous Greek mathematician Archimedes of Syracuse calculated in the third century before Christ the ratio between the height and the width of the overlap, or the "fish". He found the ratio of the great fish to be 153:265. A reference to the *vesica piscis* fits the symbolism of the duality which has to be transcended (the distance of two hundred cubits), and the central theme of the story: fish.

138

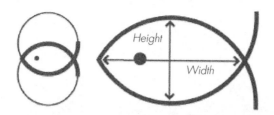

Baked fish

When the disciples arrive at the beach they see a coal fire with fish and bread on it (verse 9). Gospel stories often lavish the reader in seemingly unimportant details, while issues of perceived importance are left out. The author of this gospel tells us, for instance, that the fish was cooked on coals, while he leaves us in the dark about what Jesus looked like during this appearance.

These seemingly unimportant details, which a reader might easily miss, are nevertheless often crucial in understanding a story. In this case the burning coals refer to the story of Elijah, in which at a certain point an angel offers the prophet food that has been prepared on burning coals:

> Then he lay down under the bush and fell asleep. All at once an angel touched him and said, "Get up and eat." He looked around, and there by his head was some bread baked over hot coals, and a jar of water.
> (1 Kings 19:5-6)

We saw on page 118 that this bread baked on coals refers to the production of *amrita* in the brain. The baked fish and the bread which Jesus offers to his disciples have the same meaning. *Jesus came and ... gave it to them ...* , says verse 13. Jesus who comes to the disciples is supposed to evoke the image of the kundalini which rises to the head, and which, when arrived at the seventh chakra, feeds the person with *amrita*, or *manna*.

The fishing net

The fishing net that was not torn (verse 11) refers to a certain geometric pat-

The appearance of Jesus by the Sea of Galilee

tern that is found in many spiritual traditions as a sacred symbol. This symbol is formed from seven circles which partially overlap, as with the *vesica piscis*. This figure forms the ground pattern for all sorts of other geometric forms, such as the triangle, the square, the pentagram and the hexagram.

Seven circles as basic pattern for the hexagram

The basis figure of the seven overlapping circles can be expanded with an infinite number of these same circles. The pattern that thus emerges, and which in some spiritual traditions is regarded as the blueprint of creation, clearly reminds of a net, and certainly of a "net full of fish" (verse 11).

The disciples who are in the boat neatly fit the pattern. The author lists seven of them, and divides them into three pairs plus one (verse 2). Those of the disciples who are coupled in a duo express the basic pattern of the *vesica piscis*. Nathanael, the seventh, is from Cana, says the text, which is a subtle reference to the sacred marriage that transpired in this town (John 2:1-11). The *vesica piscis* symbolizes this sacred marriage. The boat in which the disciples are serves as the larger circle which encompasses the other seven, and completes the pattern.

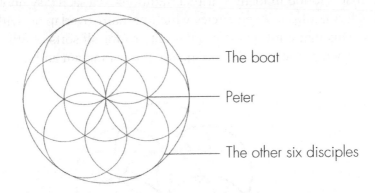

- The boat
- Peter
- The other six disciples

The right side of the boat
Jesus advises the disciples to cast the net *on* the right side of the boat, and says additionally: *and ye shall find ...* (verse 6). With this he points at a shift toward the right hemisphere of the brain.

Our rational abilities are seated in the left hemisphere, where the ego is situated. The right side takes care of – among other things – creativity, intuition, our feelings and our capacity to experience unity. When we meditate, our brain activity shifts toward the right side.
In most people, the left side is dominant, with all consequences thereof. We experience ourselves as severed from the rest of the world, which, according to Buddhism, is the basis of our suffering. The constant inner monologue of our thoughts prohibits us to make contact with our feelings and with God.

If we too want to catch one hundred and fifty three fish (that is: to experience the unity of God), like the disciples, we have to cast our net out on the right side. Said more concretely: when we close our eyes, concentrate on our inner world and let our inner monologue be, we shall find God. Jesus says it elsewhere in this way:

But when you pray, go into your room, close the door and pray to your Father, who is unseen. Then your Father, who sees what is done in secret, will reward you.
(Matt. 6:6)

142

Right after the casting out of the net on the right side of the ship, one of the disciples recognizes the resurrected Jesus, who speaks to them from the shore (verse 7). In other words: casting the net out on the other side causes a Divine experience.

Becoming like a child

Jesus addresses the disciples in verse 5 as "children." This is not simply an expression of affection. Also in John 13:3 Jesus addresses the disciples as "children," but uses another Greek word: *teknia*. The Greek *paidia* of this verse we find again in the following saying of Jesus:

> He called a little child to him, and placed the child among them. And he said: "Truly I tell you, unless you change and become like little children, you will never enter the kingdom of heaven. Therefore, whoever takes the lowly position of this child is the greatest in the kingdom of heaven.
> (Matt. 18:2-4)

Jesus speaks of becoming ego-less like a child, in order to enter the kingdom of God; making yourself "small" (making yourself "lower"), to make yourself worthy of a Divine initiation.

Stories as road signs to God

I am often asked why the Bible is so difficult to read. It requires quite a bit of knowledge of the language of images and spiritual processes to understand all symbolism in the stories. Why is not everything we should know about the way to God written straight forward?

The ingeniousness of the Bible stories is that they address every reader on his or her own level. According to your progress on the spiritual journey, you will read and understand the stories differently. Just like you yourself are peeled layer by layer during the process of purification and healing, you will discover new layers in the stories every time you re-read them. You will harvest the nutrition and advices from them which you need at that time.

Another element, of course, is that the gospels were written in another era and culture and much of the symbolism is lost on the modern reader. But you don't need to understand all the details to extract the core. The most important lessons are universal: they transcend a specific culture, *Zeitgeist* or spiritual tradition.

The stories of both the Old and the New Testament were written to explain something to us about our inner world and our personal relationship with God. The accounts of Jonah, Elijah, Peter and Jesus contain a message to us. What could this be? Read the stories and let them work on you. What touches you? What inspires you?

For the meaning of the Bible stories it isn't important whether the main character is historical or not. You say you want to find God. Do you have the courage to leave the safe ship and enter the unknown depths for this, as Jonah did? Are you prepared to carry your cross and to die to yourself, as Jesus did? Do you realize that you will have to wear a belt around your loins, just like Elijah? And if the answer to these questions is yes: how could you cast your net more on the right side of the ship, just like Peter?

The most important question, however, is the question which Jesus asks of Peter in verse 15: *do you love me more than these?* What he means with "these" is not explained, but elsewhere in the gospels Jesus is clear enough. You can't serve two masters (Matt. 6:24); it is either God or the world ... who do you love most?

> Do not love the world or anything in the world. If anyone loves the world, love for the Father is not in them.
> For everything in the world—the lust of the flesh, the lust of the eyes, and the pride of life—comes not from the Father but from the world.
> The world and its desires pass away, but whoever does the will of God lives forever.
> (1 John 2:15-17)

Epilogue

In the heart of the Jewish tradition we find the ritual immersion in a so-called *mikwah* – a bath for ritual purification. A symbolic (partial) purification plays an important role in rituals for priests and believers, but important events are marked by a full immersion. For instance when someone converts to Judaism.

It is this full immersion that John the Baptist practiced. The underlying symbolism of this "baptism" is the laying off of the old life, of the old man. The immersion symbolized a spiritual rebirth. From the water emerges a new man.

This immersion is most fundamentally a depiction of the kundalini-process. Before Jonah saves the city of Nineveh from its demise (a metaphor for spiritual awakening), he is first cast into the sea. This serves as a symbol for "being thrown" into his own subconscious; a consequence of the purifying effect of the Holy Spirit or kundalini.

In many cases the true meaning of the original Bible texts have disappeared in the process of translation, and important clues to this transformation process have been lost. For instance, the Greek word *aphesis* in the following verse, which is commonly translated as *forgiveness*, literally means "release, letting go":

> *He went into all the country around the Jordan, preaching a baptism of repentance for the forgiveness* [aphesis] *of sins.*
> (Luke 3:3, NIV)

The same word *aphesis* is in the gospels also used for the release of captives:

> *The Spirit of the Lord is upon me, Because he anointed me to preach good tidings to the poor: He hath sent me to proclaim release* [aphesis] *to the captives, And recovering of sight to the blind, To set at liberty them that are bruised …*
> (Luke 4:18, AVS)

This meaning of *aphesis* sheds a different light on the message that John the Baptist spread and confirms to us the deeper meaning of the baptism he practiced: a washing off (release) of impurities (sins).

The sea of Solomon

King Solomon had a bath for ritual purification built next to his famous temple, and in the Bible this bath is literally called a "sea". The story of the temple of Solomon is a metaphor for the person who makes a temple of himself for God to live in.[11]

The cast metal sea of Solomon (from the Holman Bible, 1890)

Just like the temple, the "sea" too is described with a huge amount of number symbolism. The first four of the twenty-two (!) verses state:

23 *He made the **Sea of cast metal**, circular in shape, measuring **ten cubits** from rim to rim and **five cubits** high. It took a line of **thirty cubits** to measure around it.*
24 *Below the rim, gourds encircled it – ten to a cubit. The gourds were cast in **two rows** in one piece with the Sea.*
25 *The Sea stood on **twelve bulls**, three facing north, three facing west, three facing south and three facing east. The Sea rested on top of them, **and their hindquarters were toward the center**.*

146

²⁶ *It was a **handbreadth** in thickness, and its rim was **like the rim of a cup,
like a lily blossom**. It held **two thousand baths**.*
(1 Kings 7:23-26)

This is an improbably large ritualistic bath – dozens of times larger than the
usual format – and is obviously bristling with symbolism.

The bath is *ten cubits from rim to rim*. Ten represents wholeness and refers
to the entire person. The height of *five cubits* – half of ten – represents the
animal nature which the bath has to purify. This is confirmed by the *twelve
bulls*, which support the bath, and which stand with *their hindquarters toward the center,* thereby emphasizing the passions of the underbelly.

The *thickness of a handbreadth* (five fingers) refers also to our lower nature.
The circumference of *thirty cubits* represents the three aspects of man that
are brought to perfection (ten): body, heart (feelings) and mind (ratio).
These three aspects are initially connected to the lower energies of the earth
(represented by the number four), which explains the division of the twelve
bulls in four groups of three.

The content of *two-thousand bath* (80,000 liters or 21,000 gallons!) is a reference to the inner duality (two) which has to be transformed to unity. The
two rows of gourds which run around the bath, represent the energy channels
ida- and *pingala-nadi*.

The rim which is shaped *like a lily blossom* is a beautiful depiction of the
crown chakra. Imported from Egypt, the lily in the Bible is what the lotus
flower is in eastern traditions. The *cup* represents the "holy grail" in the
brain, containing *amrita*, the elixir of immortality.

This gigantic water basin by the temple of Solomon not only demonstrates
how central ritualistic immersion was in Jewish tradition, but also, in an
unmistakable way, which meaning people gave it.

The baptism of Jesus
The immersion in a *mikwah* is to the Jews not only a symbol of rebirth; it

also has the meaning of a water grave. That one cannot breathe under water is undoubtedly partial to this. The baptism the way John practiced it is both a grave and a birth canal. Paul also speaks of a dying and a resurrection through *the working* (purifying and healing effect) *of God* (the kundalini):

> ... *having been buried with him in baptism, in which you were also raised with him through your faith in the working of God, who raised him from the dead.* (Colossians 2:12)

There is obviously great symbolic significance in the fact that the public life of Jesus began after his baptism by John. The old man John was discarded during the immersion in the Jordan; the new man Jesus the Christ emerged from the water.

We can now read the dialogue between John and Jesus during the baptism differently:

> 13 *Then Jesus came from Galilee to the Jordan to be baptized by John.*
> 14 *But John tried to deter him, saying,* **"I need to be baptized by you, and do you come to me?"**
> 15 *Jesus replied,* **"Let it be so now***; it is proper for us to do this to fulfill all righteousness."* **Then John consented***.*
> (Matt. 3:13-15)

Classical Greek had no punctuation such as question marks. Without the question mark, verse 14 means that John receives a baptism from God, personified in Jesus.

The Old Testament
The stories from the New Testament are in fact those of the Old Testament presented in a new way. John initiated his disciples in the mystical knowledge of the kundalini-process. From him they learned how they should actually read the Torah. After his death and per his instructions, they interwove the story of his life with the stories of the Old Testament. These stories, with which the Jews were so familiar, explained that Jesus was the Savior for which they had waited for centuries, and would initiate

those who could understand them in the inner path to the Kingdom of God.

The two best known prophets of the Old Testament, Moses and Elijah, were replaced by successors (Joshua and Elisha) when they had completed the spiritual process of God-realization. This pattern the gospel writers also applied to John the Baptist. After the baptism in the Jordan he disappears from the stage and Jesus begins his preaching.

Every spiritual tradition has its myths and legends which educate their audience about the path to spiritual awakening. The ancient Egyptians, Greeks and Romans had gods that all embodied inner aspects of man. Hinduism still has a pantheon of gods and a library of stories which teach us how we can reunite with God. In the same way, Bible stories like those of Moses, Elijah and Jonah were meant to make that which is so difficultly expressed in words understandable for the spiritual seeker.

Joshua, the awakened man
Joshua, the new name which John receives from the gospel writers, refers to the successor of Moses: Joshua, the son of Nun, which, freely translated, means "son of God."
Both Joshuas represent the awakened man but personify at a deeper level also the kundalini-energy. Jesus who heals lepers (unclean people), blind and deaf people, symbolizes the purifying and healing inner working of God.

> Just as Moses lifted up the snake in the wilderness, so the Son of Man must be lifted up, that everyone who believes may have eternal life in him."
> (John 3:14-15)

This saying of Jesus is usually seen as a prediction of his crucifixion, but if we see Jesus as personification of the kundalini, this statement becomes a beautiful message for us: we must lead the Divine "serpent" upward to the crown chakra, so that we too achieve eternal life with God.

Jesus' death on the cross shows how the old man must die. Just like Jonah,

After the death of Jesus the disciples, filled with the Holy Spirit, continue to baptize converts.
A ritual (sacrament) which is still central to Christianity.

Jesus stays three days in the grave, to teach us that the light of God can only come to live in us after a journey through the darkness. Jesus' passion symbolizes the process of working through unresolved emotions; all the pain that has to be embraced before the ego can be discarded.

John the Baptist first personally experienced this process of awakening, and then expressed it publically in the gospel stories as Jesus, with his crucifixion en resurrection.
He died a very painful and humiliating death by the hands of those who couldn't see the light of God in him, and afterward joined himself to his Father by means of a resurrection body, which we also can obtain.

Conclusion
By building bridges between traditions I aim to demonstrate that all religious differences are mere variations on the same brilliant truth. Just like all branches need the whole tree to exist, so should we cherish our heritage as part of the greater dynamic of tradition and insight. I sincerely hope that my work will help to turn the tide of declining church attendance and that Christianity will regain relevance to the younger generations.

The beautiful church buildings, the inspired and dedicated priests and ministers, the liturgy with her powerful rituals; they are of inestimable value to the spiritual seeker. Christianity too has been given the ears and eyes to perceive what Jesus said about the inner process of spiritual maturation. A global revolution in the way in which people see God is at hand – not as some distant ruler who demands obedience and homage, but as a Beloved who stands at the door of our hearts, waiting and yearning for us to be ready for the sacred marriage.

The gospel writers had good reasons to rewrite the life story of John the Baptist, including giving him another name. However, they also went through considerable lengths, particularly the authors Luke and John, to leave clues that John the Baptist was the Christ. Luke even goes so far that he ascribes the Lord's Prayer to John the Baptist:

One day Jesus was praying in a certain place. When he finished, one of his disciples said to him, **"Lord, teach us to pray, just as John taught his disciples."**
He said to them, "When you pray, say:
"'Father, hallowed be your name, your kingdom come. Give us each day our daily bread.
Forgive us our sins, for we also forgive everyone who sins against us. And lead us not into temptation."
(Luke 11:1-4)

All the clues were left to be discovered when the time would be right. It is my conviction that this time is now.

Appendix Paintings with a John-is-Jesus code

The Holy Family, by William-Adolphe Bouguereau, 1863.
Private collection.

The 2=1-code in the fingers of Maria.

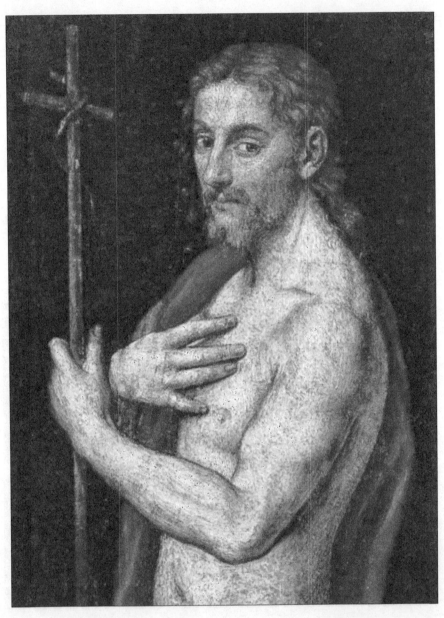

John the Baptist, by Giovanni Francesco Caroto, early 16th century.
Private collection.

John has the appearance of Jesus. He holds a wooden cross without a banner.

Madonna with Child, by Francesco di Stefano, also known as Pesellino, ca. 1450 – 1500. Bardini Museum, Florence, Italy.

John has the *Ecce Agnus Dei*-banner in his hand and points not to Jesus but to himself and Maria. The infant Jesus displays two fingers (the 2=1-code).

Madonna with Child and John the Baptist, by Andrea del Sarto, 1486-1530.
Galleria Borghese, Rome.

Mary and Jesus both point to John. Jesus and John appear similar.

Saint John the Baptist, by Andrea del Sarto, about 1517.
Worcester Art Museum, Worcester, US.

Johns points at a wooden cross without a banner. The wreath of vine leaves around his head symbolizes the kundalini process. The divine energy is often associated with vines and with wine in the gospels.

The Holy Family of the Oak Tree, by Raphael, ca. 1518.
Museo del Prado, Madrid, Spain.

John displays the *Ecce Agnus Dei*-banner. The infant Jesus has put his hand on the shoulder of John and points at the banner. Both children stand with one foot on the manger.

The Esterhazy Madonna, by Raphael, 1508.
Museum of Fine Arts, Budapest.

John looks at the *Ecce Agnus Dei*-banner and Jesus points at John.
The banner also wraps around the belly and head of John.

159

St. John the Baptist in the Wilderness, by Raphael, circa 1517.
Louvre Museum, Paris, France.

John points at a wooden cross seemingly coming from a tree. A tree is a universal metaphor for the kundalini energy. He is holding the *Ecce Agnus Dei*-banner in his hand: he is the Lamb of God.

St John the Baptist in the desert, by Raphael, 1518-1520.
Galleria Degli Uffizi (Uffizi Gallery), Florence, Italy.

John points at a wooden cross fastened to a tree. A tree is a universal metaphor for the kundalini energy. The cross radiates divine light flowing from the tree, thereby connecting the two metaphors: Jesus' crucifixion is in the gospel a metaphor for a kundalini-awakening.

The Manchester Madonna (uncompleted), by Michelangelo, ca. 1497.
National Gallery, London.

John has placed one hand on Jesus, and shows with his other hand two fingers (the 2=1-code).
The four angels in the background are grouped in twos, through which the 2=1-symbolism is
even more accentuated. The two angels behind John hold a document of some sort over him,
which they read together. Could it be the Ecce Agnus Dei-banner?

The Doni Tondo, by Michelangelo, 1506-1508.
Galleria degli Uffizi, Florence, Italy.

John and Jesus look nearly identical. John carries a cross without banner and looks up to two boys standing in an intimate embrace. Like Jesus and John, one boy is naked and the other wears a brown garment, thus symbolizing that Jesus and John are one.

The Vision of Saint Jerome, by Girolamo Francesco Maria Mazzola, known as Parmigianino, 1503–1540.
National Gallery, London, United Kingdom.

John the Baptist points with the fingers of his right hand both to himself and to the infant Jesus. He holds a wooden cross without a banner. Both Maria and Jesus display the 2=1-code with their fingers.

St John the Baptist in the Desert, by Francisco Collantes, 1630.
State Hermitage Museum, St. Petersburg.

John the Baptist – in the foreground – wears both a brown garment (made from animal hair) and a red robe. In the background, John baptizes Jesus, while still wearing the brown garment. The red robe now lies next to Jesus, as he has disrobed for his baptism. John holds a wooden cross without a banner.

Baptism of Christ, by Elisabetta Sirani, 1658.
The Church San Girolamo Della Certosa in Bologna, Italy.

Jesus and John look the same. Their robes have different colors. Beside them stands a man who wears both colors and who points at John. Above them hovers an angel who also wears a combination of the two colors. John holds a wooden cross without a banner.

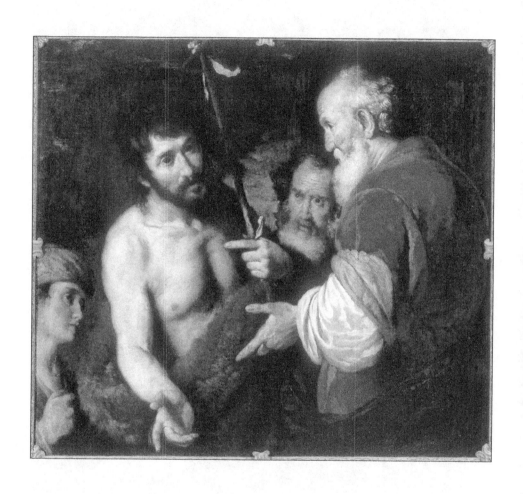

Saint John the Baptist Interrogated about Christ, by Bernardo Strozzi, 1618-1620.
National Trust, Kedleston Hall and Eastern Museum, Kedleston, Great Britain.

John points at himself with the same hand in which he holds the *Ecce Agnus Dei*-banner.

167

Coronation of the Virgin with Sts John the Baptist, Peter and Paul, by Girolamo del Pacchia, 1513.
Santo Spirito Church, Siena, Italy.

Jesus and John look as good as the same. John holds the *Ecce Agnus Dei*-banner, and Peter
(the central figure) points at John.

The Madonna and Child with Saint John the Baptist, Saint Paul and Saint Hyacinth,
by Bevilacqua, 1580–1594.
Harvington Hall, Harvington, Great Britain.

John appears to point at the *Ecce Agnus Dei*-banner, but the shadow of his finger shows that he
points at himself.

John the Baptist, Florentine School, Italy, 16th century.
Private collection.

John points with one hand to the cross (without a banner) and with the other to himself.

The Madonna and Child with Saint John the Baptist and Saint Jerome, Venetian School, Italy,
16th century.
Gunby Hall Estate, Gunby, Great Britain.

The infant Jesus points to John. John points to the Bible. He holds a wooden cross without a
banner. In front of John stands an ornament with three small pillars, upon which Mary has placed
her hand: symbol for the three energy courses which are involved in a kundalini-awakening?

St. John in the Desert, by Domenico Veneziano, ca. 1445.
National Gallery of Art, Washington, United States of America.

John takes off his garment of camel's hair and puts on the (red) garment of Christ. The ascending mountain path, which is emphasized by the loose pebbles, represents the (narrow) way to God, which John has traveled.

The Baptism of Christ, by Tintoretto, 1585.
Musei Capitolini, Rome, Italy.

Johns holds a wooden cross without a banner. The dove of the Holy Spirit hovers over both men and the divine light shines on John instead of Jesus.

The Baptism of Christ, by Adam Elsheimer, ca. 1599.
National Gallery, London, England.

John and Jesus look nearly identical. The dove of the Holy Spirit hovers over both men and the divine light shines on John instead of Jesus.

The Baptism of Jesus Christ, by Giovanni Battista Crespi, known as Il Cerano, 1601.
Städelsches Kunstinstitut und Städtische Galerie, Frankfurt am Main, Germany.

The dove of the Holy Spirit is positioned between John and Jesus. John carries a wooden cross without banner. Jesus lacks color and has a ghostlike appearance. In the below right corner lies a piece of paper with text on it. A hint that the painting contains a message?

Virgin of the Rocks, by Leonardo da Vinci, 1483–1486.
Musée du Louvre, Paris, France.

John and Jesus look nearly identical.
The angel holds Jesus with one hand and points at John with the other.

The Baptism of Christ, by Mattia Preti, circa 1695.
La Valletta National Museum Of Fine Arts, Malta.

The dove of the Holy Spirit hovers over John instead of Jesus. The body of John casts a shadow on the face of Jesus, revealing that the divine light shines on John.

The Baptism of Christ, by Mattia Preti, 1661.
St John's Co-Cathedral, Valletta, Malta.

John has a central position in the painting.
The dove of the Holy Spirit hovers over him instead of Jesus.

Saint John the Baptist, anonymous, 15th century.
National Gallery, Bologna, Italy.

John holds the *Ecce Agnus Dei*-banner and points to himself.

St. John the Baptist, by Jacob Jordaens, circa 1617.
Columbus Museum of Art, Columbus, US.

John holds the *Ecce Agnus Dei*-banner. He points at the banner and at himself.

The Holy Family with John the Baptist as a Boy and Saint Elizabeth, by Giulio Clovio,
1556-1557.
Museo Lázaro Galdiano, Madrid, Spain.

John's mother, Elizabeth, uses her body to prevent John from seeing Maria and Jesus, thus
symbolizing that Maria and Jesus exist within John.

Madonna and Child and the Young St John the Baptist, by Sandro Botticelli, 1495.
Palazzo Pitti, Florence, Italy.

The faces of John en Jesus are pressed together, forming one face.
A wooden cross without banner is positioned between them.

Holy Trinity with Mary Magdalene, John the Baptist and Tobias and the Angel,
by Sandro Botticelli, 1491–1493.
Courtauld Institute of Art, London, England.

John and Jesus look nearly identical. John holds a cross without a banner.

Madonna and Christ Child with Infant Saint John Baptist and Three Angels,
by Domenico Ghirlandaio, 1485-1494.
Birmingham Museum of Art, Alabama, USA.

Except for one angel, all look at John instead of Jesus. John holds a cross without a banner.

Saint John the Baptist (San Giovanni Battista), by Alvise Vivarini, 1475.
Thyssen-Bornemisza Museum, Madrid, Spain.

Johns points at a wooden cross without a banner.

St John the Baptist, by Guercino, circa 1645.
Capitoline Museums, Rome, Italy.

Johns holds a wooden cross. He is reading the banner with *Ecce Agnus Dei*:
he is the Lamb of God.

The Young Saint John the Baptist, by Pierro di Cosimo, circa 1500.
The Met Fifth Avenue, New York, United States of America.

The cross in front of John is made of reed. Because of its hollow stem, reed is used in the Bible as a metaphor for the spine in which the divine energy of the Holy Spirit flows.

Saint John the Baptist, by Perugino (Pietro di Cristoforo Vannucci), circa 1500.
The Met Fifth Avenue, New York, United States of America.

Johns points at a wooden cross without a banner.

Saint John the Baptist, by El Greco, circa 1600.
Museu de Belles Arts de València, Valencia, Spain.

John holds a wooden cross without a banner.
With his other hand he points at the lamb and at himself.

The burial of count Orgaz, by El Greco, 1586.
Iglesia de Santo Tomé, Toledo, Spain.

John and Jesus look at each other. Their arms form an oval suggesting a certain intimacy.
They look nearly identical.

John the Baptist, by Paolo Morando, known as Cavazzola, 16e century.
The Civic Museum of Castelvecchio, Verona, Italy.

John has the appearance of Jesus. He holds a cross with a few olive leaves connected to it. Because olive oil is used for anointing in the Bible, tradition connects the olive tree to the tree of eternal life from the garden of Eden, which stands for the "kundalini tree".

St John the Baptist, by Jacopo del Sellaio, circa 1485.
Museum of Fine Arts, Budapest, Hungary.

John holds a cross, the banner is in his hand. He points at a barren tree with an axe in its trunk: the tree of good and evil from the garden of Eden. Around the tree spirals a vine: a metaphor for the kundalini energy, flowing upward to the brain.

Saint John the Baptist preaching, by Luca Giordano, 1695.
Los Angeles County Museum of Art, Los Angeles, United States of America.

John has the appearance of Jesus. The wooden cross (without banner) in his hand parallels the tree behind him, subtly connecting the cross with the (kundalini) tree.

Saint John the Baptist in the Wilderness, by Michelangelo Merisi, called Caravaggio, circa 1604.
Nelson-Atkins Museum of Art, Kansas City, US.

John holds a cross without a banner. It is made of reed. Because of its hollow stem, reed is used in the bible as a metaphor for the spine in which the divine energy of the Holy Spirit flows.

Madonna and Child, Saint John the Baptist and Saint George, by Paris Bordone, early 1530s.
Pushkin State Museum of Fine Arts, Moscow, Russia.

John carries a cross without a banner. He holds the hand of the infant Jesus. The infant is partly "hidden" behind the scarf of his mother, indicating that it symbolizes the Christ child within John.

The Baptism of Christ, by Paris Bordone, 1535-1540.
National Gallery of Art, Washington, US.

John is standing with his back against a large tree, holding it with one hand, thereby indicating that the baptism symbolizes a kundalini awakening in his the spine.

Riposo sulla via del ritorno dall'Egitto, by Paris Bordone, circa 1540.
National Gallery of Scotland, Edinburgh.

The faces of John and Jesus are so close that they seem to become one face.
John holds the Ecce Agnus Dei-banner in his hand, indicating that he is the Lamb of God.

The Baptism of Christ, by Annibale Carracci, 1585.
Santi Gregorio e Siro, Bologna, Italy.

The dove of the Holy Spirit is positioned between John en Jesus. John holds a wooden cross conspicuously in front of Jesus, thereby lining up the dove, the baptism cup and the cross, connecting them in the symbolism of the event. The bystander on the left displays with his hands the 2=1-code.

The Baptism of Christ, by Piero della Francesca, 1440–1450.
National Gallery, London, England.

The man undressing next to John is subtly connected with him at elbow level: where the upper arm of the anonymous man ends, the lower arm of John begins. The man pulling off his robe expresses the deeper meaning of the baptism: the change of John in Jesus. His face is covered by his clothes, reinforcing the symbolism of an identity change. A tree is positioned on the top of his head, hinting at a kundalini awakening.

Notes

(1) See my book *Ecce Homo* page 50-61

(2) See my book *Kundalini Awakening*

(3) See my book *Kundalini Awakening* page 93-94

(4) See my book *Kundalini Awakening* page 159

(5) See my book *Kundalini Awakening* page 101-109

(6) See my book *Kundalini Awakening* page 135

(7) See my book *Kundalini Awakening* page 178-179

(8) See my book *Ecce Homo* page 98-103

(9) See my book *Kundalini Awakening* page 105-107

(10) See my book *Ecce Homo* page 110-113

(11) See my book *Kundalini Awakening* p 113-121

Sources

This book makes use of four different English translation of the Bible, depending on the specialty of each translation and the nature of the discussion at hand.

Used websites
www.biblos.com
(Greek and Hebrew source texts of the Bible)

www.ancient-hebrew.org
(Ancient Hebrew characters and their meaning)

www.abarim-publications.com
(Biblical names and their meanings, and studies in Biblical Hebrew and Greek)

Attributions

MAGDALENA
PUBLISHERS

Colophon

John the Baptist who became Jesus the Christ© was written by Anne-Marie Wegh.
www.anne-marie.eu
www.johnbecamejesus.com

The cover and layout of this book were designed by Marc Boom.

ISB-nummer 978-90-825023-1-2
NUR: 708

Cover image: The Virgin, the Baby Jesus and Saint John the Baptist, by William-Adolphe Bouguereau, 1875 (private collection).

The first edition of this book was produced in the spring of 2017.

John the Baptist who became Jesus the Christ© was published by Magdalena Publishers.

Magdalena Publishers
Kerkpad 4a
6631 AB Horssen
The Netherlands
Telefoon 0031 6-54 68 34 27

WWW.ANNE-MARIE.EU

Made in the USA
Middletown, DE
18 October 2023

41017826R00117